The Stewardship Model™

By

Michael D. Fluker

Cover Painting by Greg Rumph, II

Rhapsody
PUBLICATIONS

Rhapsody Publications, Inc. P.O. Box 991 Tallevast, FL 34270

Library of Congress Control Number 2002115282
ISBN 0-9787740-1-9
Printed in the U.S.A.

The Stewardship Model™

Contents

Thank you, Lord Jesus, for giving me this opportunity to share with the world the gifts you gave me. When I felt weak, you strengthened me; when I wanted to quit, you encouraged me to go on. You told me that the victory was mine, and I still believe you. I will strive daily to fulfill this calling you have placed on me, that I may hear You say, "Well done, thou good and faithful servant."

To my wife, Julie, I'm nothing without you, and everything with you. I know it wasn't easy spending so many late nights and early mornings apart, while I composed this book, but you persevered, and I appreciate and thank you for your love and support.

To my parents, John Ellis and Janette Graham, thank you for being wise voices and constant support in all that I do. To my rock, my grandmother, Georgia Cook, you said that I could do anything I put my mind to, and I still hear those words every day. Words can't express what you mean to me. To my brother, Corey Graham, I love you, and the door is now open for you to do great things.

A heartfelt "Thank you" goes out to my Pastor, Bishop Henry L. Porter, and Westcoast for your advice and guidance. Your wisdom has opened doors I could not see.

I would like to thank all of my friends who contributed to this project. To DeWayne Harvey, thanks for helping me lay my financial foundation. To my buddy, Clara Cross, thanks for your daily sermons, making sure that I didn't grow discouraged by this daunting task. To Derrek Gunnells, thanks for reaching out to help me during my time of need. I also would like to extend warm thanks to Lawrence Jones, Mrs. A.B. Jones, Patricia Ellis, Russell Thomas, Bishop E.M. Wortham, Evangelist Timothy Riley, Reverend Kelvin Lumpkin, Mother Delores Lumpkin, Wanda Floyd, Michelle Clark, Vicke Mack, Gregory Rumph, II, Michael White, Rev. Florine Daniels, Vernon Firestone and Julie Ann Howell: your words and contributions encouraged me more than you will ever know.

Thanks to my editor, Elizabeth Hoffmann, for being the answer to my prayers, and to Elmer and Wanda Norris, for editorial support.

Finally, to everyone else who supported me by prayer, fasting, and encouragement, thank you.

I DEDICATE THIS BOOK
IN LOVING MEMORY OF
MY GRANDFATHER, RICHARD COOK

PREFACE

We live in an age where computers are making the world smaller; trips to the stars are seen almost as a common part of life. Opportunities for prosperity still abound in America despite the recent economic uncertainty. There are more millionaires in America now than at any other point in American history.

With all of these incredible accomplishments, I was embarrassed to ask myself, "Why are so many people still poor and unfulfilled?" I didn't know the answer, so I began to study and research. I wanted to know why there are some people who are extremely talented, yet have no money, and some who have talents most would deem simple yet are rich beyond their wildest dreams.

For example, a visiting speaker once told me a story about a woman he knew who baked delicious pies. She would bake them for him. One day he suggested that she sell those pies. She refused, reasoning that the pies wouldn't sell. After much convincing and encouragement she began to sell the pies. She sold out the first batch. The more she baked, and offered for sale, the more people would buy. The demand grew so that she had no choice but to start a corporation. This corporation grew and grew until the woman began to sell the pies in grocery stores.

What's my point? How does a woman turn a seemingly common talent like baking pies into a successful corporation? She learns how to be a good steward.

Being A Steward

When talking about stewardship you must be aware that it involves more than the sound use of money. It involves identifying who you are, what you do, and how to do it so that it benefits those around you. Stewardship is the process by which God shares His gifts to the world through the use of your talents and abilities. Therefore, being a good steward is the highest order of your life, because you are enabling God to share His blessings with others through you. You are a steward whether you possess one talent or ten. Good stewardship takes that talent and helps you use it to benefit yourself and the world.

After I identified stewardship as a natural progression to prosperity, I felt that people needed a model identifying key steps they could follow to prosper. So I created The Stewardship Model, an exciting, unique, and revolutionary tool which provides an in-depth view of the principal components of stewardship, divided into two parts, personal and financial.

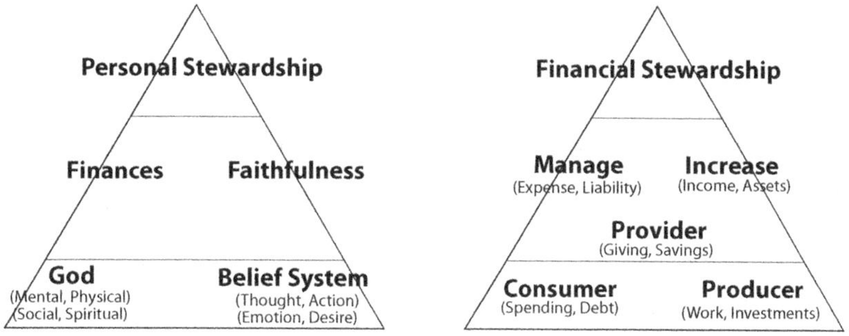

Personal Stewardship Personal stewardship involves the way you manage and increase yourself. There are two components of personal stewardship.

The first part involves the identification of your moneymaking talent or ability. For example, have you identified your talents? If so, have you established an improvement program to develop them?

The second part deals with the way you think/feel about your talents and abilities once they have been identified. This greatly influences your belief or lack of belief in the value of your talent.

Some questions you might ask yourself include:

a) What is my thinking pattern?
b) Do I commonly think positive thoughts about myself, my skills, and my abilities, or am I burdened with a negative thinking pattern?
c) Do I have a desire to share my talent with the world?

Your success or failure in personal stewardship has a direct effect on your success or failure as a financial steward.

Financial Stewardship Financial stewardship involves management and increase of the money in your possession. There are two components of financial stewardship.

Part one deals with the way you manage your cash flow. For example, do you have a financial plan? Do you have financial goals, or is your spending out of control and resulting in excessive debt?

Part two covers investment or increase of your money. Do you have a plan to increase your money on your journey to prosperity? Your success or failure in financial stewardship can be measured by your success or failure in managing and increasing the money you have.

As we seek to be wise stewards of the finances in our possession, we must see money beyond our present viewpoint. Whether we recognize it or not, money affects our lives beyond the present way we view it. We must not be as those who see, but never percieve; those who hear, but never understand (see Isaiah 6:9).

Chapter 1
Stewardship

There are many books claiming they provide knowledge on growing wealthy. Some take an approach which focuses on sound financial management. Others focus on giving as a means for increase. Still others claim investing leads to wealth. Each of these has its place. I believe that the path to wealth encompasses these basic thoughts: management and increase. The Bible calls this stewardship. I define stewardship as the continual management and increase in the use of skills, time, abilities, and resources to share God's gifts with the world. The Bible presents an example of stewardship in a parable located in Matthew 25:14-28. It reads as follows:

v14 "Again, it will be like a man going on a journey, who called his servants and entrusted his property to them.
v15 "To one he gave five talents of money, to another two talents, and to another one talent, each according to his ability. Then he went on his journey.
v16 "The man who had received the five talents went at once and put his money to work and gained five more.
v17 "So also, the one with the two talents gained two more.
v18 "But the man who had received the one talent went off, dug a hole in the ground and hid his master's money.
v19 "After a long time the master of those servants returned and settled accounts with them.
v20 "The man who had received the five talents brought the other five. 'Master,' he said, 'you entrusted me with five talents. See, I have gained five more.'
v21 "His master replied, 'Well done, good and faithful servant! You have been faithful with a few things; I will put you in charge of many things. Come and share your master's happiness!'

v22 "The man with the two talents also came. 'Master,' he said, 'you entrusted me with two talents; see, I have gained two more.'
v23 "His master replied, 'Well done, good and faithful servant! You have been faithful with a few things; I will put you in charge of many things. Come and share your master's happiness!'
v24 "Then the man who had received the one talent came. 'Master,' he said, 'I knew that you are a hard man, harvesting where you have not sown and gathering where you have not scattered seed.
v25 "'So I was afraid and went out and hid your talent in the ground. See, here is what belongs to you.'
v26 "His master replied, 'You wicked, lazy servant! So you knew that I harvest where I have not sown and gather where I have not scattered seed?
v27 "'Well then, you should have put my money on deposit with the bankers, so that when I returned I would have received it back with interest.'
v28 "'Take the talent from him and give it to the one who has the ten talents'". (NIV)

Let's look more closely at verse 16. The verse says that the man took his money and put it to work and gained five more. He used what he was given to increase. The story of the second servant emphasizes the value of investing wisely and earning the same proportion of increase, though the amount of increase is smaller. The benefits of being a good steward are evidenced in verse 21. "Well done, good and faithful servant! You have been faithful with a few things; I will put you in charge of many things. Come and share you master's happiness!" You become wealthy!!

The Stewardship Model

As I wrote in the Preface, after I identified stewardship as a natural progression to prosperity, I felt that people could benefit from a model identifying key steps they could follow to prosper. So, I created the Stewardship Model. The Stewardship Model is an exciting, unique, and revolutionary tool which provides an in-depth view of the principal components of stewardship. The Stewardship Model is composed of two components: personal stewardship and financial stewardship. Both of these are made possible by time stewardship.

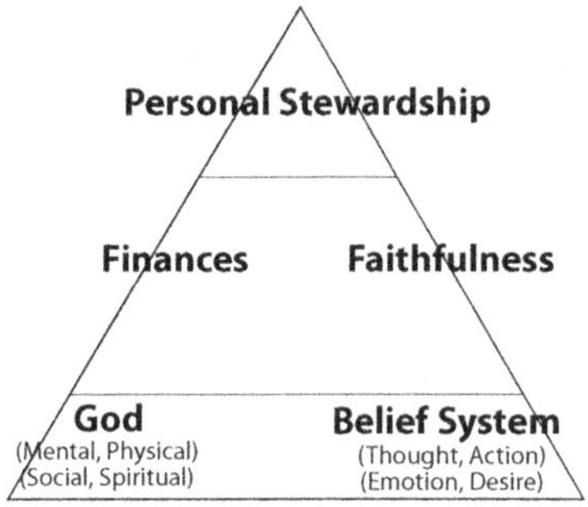

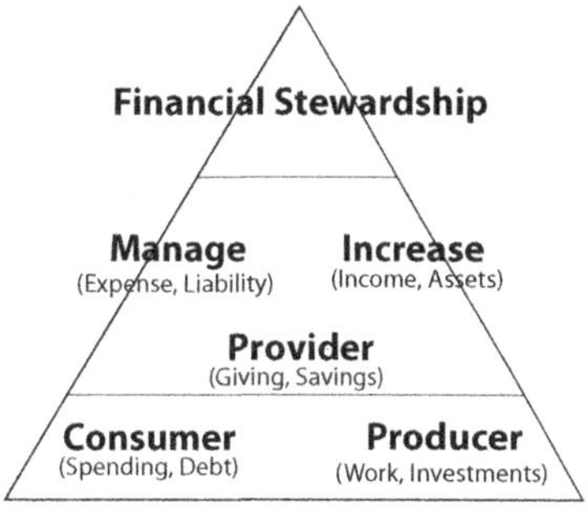

Time Stewardship Why do some people get more done than others with similar skills and abilities? One chief reason, I believe, is that people who are successful more often than others value their time. The majority of their time is not wasted on those things which are of no real benefit to them. By "of no real benefit" I mean not consistent with their established mission in life. Excessive television or other forms of recreation are time-wasters.

Personal Stewardship Personal stewardship involves how you manage and increase yourself. There are two parts to personal stewardship. The first part involves the identification of your moneymaking talent or ability. The second part deals with the way you think/feel about your talents and abilities, once they have been identified. This greatly influences your belief or lack of belief in the value of your talent. Our talents are extremely valuable because each of our talents is unique. As our awareness of our talent grows, we move to another level.

However, many of you experience a difficult time using this talent to benefit yourself and others, because you don't see it as something valuable people are willing to pay money for. Still others compare themselves to someone else who may have a similar talent, allowing fear and doubt to prevent use of their talent.

The Bible confirms this in the Parable of the Talents. The Bad Steward was aware of his talent. He was a trader just like the others. But after comparing himself to the others he felt that the Master was a hard man and that his talent was not sufficient to increase the Master's money. If you were aware how worthy your talent is, you would begin to believe in yourself through a positive attitude (like the other stewards in this parable).

Financial Stewardship Financial stewardship involves management and increase of the money in your possession. There are two components of financial stewardship.

Part one deals with how you manage your money. Part two covers investment or increase of your money.

As I have discussed thus far, management and increase form the foundation of stewardship. An understanding of these terms is essential in prospering through stewardship.

Windows of Stewardship

Management is defined as the use of time, abilities, and money to meet your physical needs, wants, obligations, and provision for others.

Increase is defined as the use of time, abilities, and/or money, to increase money or proficiency. Increase means growth in something.

Each person on the planet views stewardship through what I call the Windows of Stewardship.

I. Manage & Increase
II. Manage & No Increase
III. No Manage & Increase
IV. No Manage & No Increase

Below are examples of how time, abilities, and finances are viewed through the Windows of Stewardship.

Time Stewardship

I. Manage & Increase - The Good Steward Successful stewards assign a monetary and personal value to all 24 hours of each day. They realize that to maximize their income and their lives in general they have to assign a value to their time. For example, if you want to become any type of professional, then you can't spend more time watching television than you do practicing your trade.

Stewards who view their time as valuable save time through proper management, to develop and maintain relationships, take care of their bodies, nourish their spiritual lives, and much more. In other words, practice what you want to happen. Consistent time invested from your schedule to discover your talents and sharpen them is essential for successful stewardship.

II. Manage & No Increase - The Efficient Steward Do you know people who manage time so well that they believe that getting things done is much more important to them than practicing their skills or abilities? Are you this type of individual? You make time to exercise; you have time for the kids, your friends, even feeding your spiritual man. But you don't practice your abilities or skills. You remain the same . . . very efficient. You are burying your talent in a hole. Remember the parable. The good stewards immediately went out and traded with others (practiced), while the bad steward didn't practice; in fact he buried his talent in a hole, as many of us do.

III. No Manage & Increase - The Effective Steward Practice is the key to increasing your talent. But what happens when practice becomes such a great part of your life that you don't manage your time? For example, there was a period in my life that I was labeled a "workaholic," someone who spends an inordinate amount of time working or practicing his or her skill or ability. I was very diligent in practice. I practiced all the time. I studied, and I became very skillful in what I was doing at the time. But, due to improper eating habits and lack of exercise, my health suffered. My relationships, once thriving, began to suffer. My friends, even my family, were suffering because I was always studying or practicing. Even my spiritual life was dry.

IV. No Manage & No Increase - The Lazy Steward Surprisingly, many people have no control of how they use their time. It's controlled by outside sources (other people, television, excessive recreation). However you spend your time makes someone wealthy. There is a relationship between time and money. If you spend all your time at the movies, the movie people get rich. If you spend all of your time buying and listening to music, the people in the music industry grow rich. See my point? Because you are spending your time on those pursuits, you don't allot time for discovering your talent, and/or establishing the habit of practice. As you have discovered, management (setting and following priorities) and increase (practice) are important components of Time Stewardship.

Personal Stewardship

I. Manage & Increase - The Good Steward What a joy it is to know why you were placed on Earth! Each of us has some talent to offer others. That is what managing yourself is all about. By seeking our talent, we acknowledge our responsibility to contribute to the world. Positive belief is the vehicle which transports our talent to the world. The way the good steward feels about his talent is comparable to the way the Word of God felt to Jeremiah, "like a burning fire shut up in my bones" (Jeremiah 20:9, NKJV). These stewards believe that no matter how great the world is now around them, it will be better once they contribute their talent, whether great or small.

II. Manage & No Increase - The Efficient Steward The Efficient Steward has discovered his talent. He knows who he is and what he has to offer. The problem is he doesn't believe that anyone else is interested in his talent. Please see the Preface for the story about a lady who changed her mind about her pie-making ability.

III. No Manage & Increase - The Effective Steward The effective steward desires to impact the world. His problem is he doesn't know how.

He has endless dreams of greatness but has not developed the desire to discover what he has to offer. He impresses others with his grand dreams and aspirations, but he fails to impact the world, because he believes that his impact on the world is based on who he is, not on what he has to offer.

IV. No Manage & No Increase - The Lazy Steward The most desperate of situations belongs to the lazy steward. This steward has no interest in discovering what he has to offer. He's quite comfortable just passing through life. He feels that he has nothing to offer anyway, so why bother? He's quite satisfied working nine to five at whatever job pays the most money, regardless of the job's lack of stimulation and fulfillment. The lazy steward believes that he doesn't possess any talent. Satan has tricked him. Satan can't steal talent. Satan tries to deceive each person into believing that the person's talent is worthless. Once Satan deceives the steward into the belief that the steward's talent can't earn money, the talent begins to wane from lack of practice.

As your talent level decreases, opportunities fade away also because opportunities require a certain skill level. The fading of opportunities further "reinforces" the belief that your ability is worthless.

Financial Stewardship

I. Manage & Increase - The Good Steward Rare is the individual who realizes the necessity to manage money and seek to create and/or increase. These individuals truly live the abundant life. They have realized that wealth begins with contentment and continues with increase. Many people will never be wealthy no matter how much money they make. Why? Because they are never content.

Contentment simply means an uncomplaining acceptance of the money you have. For most people this is not the case. Their expenses expand to fill whatever vacuum is created by an increase in income. In their own minds they never make enough money. The more money they make, the more money they feel they need.

If you are not content, then you can't live beneath your means, which is a key component to managing your money to grow wealthy. Wealth by definition means having more than enough money. So if you are unable to live beneath your means, then it's possible to earn millions of dollars and still want more because you feel that what you have is not enough, even though your needs are met. That's not wealth, that's greed.

Contentment and greed are conditions of the heart. One of these conditions concerning money is present in the heart of every human being, Christians included. Unconvinced? Then listen to what the Bible talks about in James 4:3: "You ask and do not receive, because you ask amiss, that you may spend it [money] on your pleasures" (NKJV). Simple and straight to the point. James is saying that one reason you may not have what you want is that you are greedy and would use the money on your own pleasures.

Individuals who are content with managing and increasing their money are open to opportunities which may come their way to increase their money, but they are not unceasingly striving to increase their money. Typically, these people live within their means with contentment and discretion while focusing a portion of their energies toward increase, whether it be investing, or owning a business, etc. This is the epitome of the Stewardship Model. These stewards are the ones who are blessed with more and retain it.

II. Manage & No Increase - The Efficient Steward These stewards are so content that they don't strive for more. Sometimes they associate riches with problematic lives or unrighteousness. For whatever reason, whether lack of knowledge or lack of desire, these stewards don't increase their wealth. They live life not according to spiritual principles, and they expect their financial situation to remain the same. Unfortunately for them, that doesn't happen. We live in a changing environment. Spouses die, children are born, and people get sick or lose jobs or experience other losses. Without the ability to create, the ability to manage means nothing. Eventually this person loses to others what he once had as Matthew 25:29 says: "For unto everyone that hath shall be given, and he shall have abundance: but from him that hath not [increases not] shall be taken away even that which he hath" (KJV).

III. No Manage & Increase - The Effective Steward These stewards have the ability and desire to increase. Their downfall is the lack of financial management. As did the prodigal son, these have much and can spend much with reckless abandon. Their personal lives suffer. They don't pay their bills. They are in debt. They don't save. They don't plan how to manage what they create. Basically, these are the ones who earn above-average incomes, for example $80,000.00, but ride around town in a $50,000.00 foreign car, possess a $10,000.00/year wardrobe, and take vacations amounting to thousands of dollars. Because these individuals don't manage, they easily live above their means. They are one emergency away from disaster. Proverbs 27:23-24 teaches, "Be thou diligent to know the state of thy flocks, and look well to thy herds. For riches are not for ever: and doth the crown endure to every generation?" (KJV).

IV. No Manage & No Increase - The Lazy Steward The lazy stewards are unable to manage and have no desire to manage. They bury their money in the hole by using up their resources and trying to borrow from others. They can very quickly lose all. The inability to manage contributes to their decrease. The inability to increase prevents the replenishing of what results from the inability to manage. Fear is their motivator. People who don't manage or increase are trapped in the ever-descending spiral to poverty.

Establishing True Stewardship

There is hope. An individual operating in windows II-IV can be freed. The first step is to learn how to change the things you directly influence. Chief among these is the management of your existing time, skills, abilities, and resources. In spite of the hardship, your existing debt, etc., you are the one who receives the resources. You are the one held accountable for the use of them. You are the one in possession of them. You must regain control of your time and control of your money from debt, impulse spending, or any other area which seeks to limit your money. There are three principles one should remember regarding true stewardship. The Bible provides examples of these principles of true stewardship in Matthew 25:16-18, 22-23, 25, and 28 (NIV).

v16 "The man who had received the five talents went at once and put his money to work and gained five more.
v17 "So also, the one with the two talents gained two more.
v18 "But the man who had received the one talent went off, dug a hole in the ground and hid his master's money."
v22 "The man with the two talents also came. 'Master,' he said, 'you entrusted me with two talents; see, I have gained two more.'
v23 'His master replied, 'Well done, good and faithful servant! You have been faithful with a few things; I will put you in charge of many things. Come and share your master's happiness!'"
v25 "'So I was afraid and went out and hid your talent in the ground. See, here is what belongs to you.'"
v28 "'Take the talent from him, and give it to the one who has the ten talents.'"

Three Principles of True Stewardship

The first principle is called **Act or Be Acted Upon**. We have a tendency to wait until fear goes away before we act. As most of us are well aware, the fear doesn't go away; it acts upon us, preventing us from doing what we desire to do.

I had the idea for this book in my head for nearly a year before I began to write. I was afraid that no one would buy the book, that it would not help anyone, that I wouldn't be able to finance the publishing, and so forth and so on. Needless to say, these doubts and fears acted upon me, delaying the completion of a book I knew God wanted me to complete. I wanted to wait until those problems were solved before I acted, but the fear didn't go away. Actually, I began to feel worse because I wasn't doing what I knew I was supposed to do. I was burying my talent in the ground like the slothful servant (Matthew 25:25) who was afraid and allowed his fear to act upon him, causing him to bury the master's talent in the ground. Had I chosen to respond like the good stewards (vv. 16-17) and immediately begun writing, I would not have allowed those negative thoughts an opportunity to exert their influence over me for nearly a year, and I would have reaped the positive feeling that comes from doing what you are called to do. If we don't act, that is, move toward the thing or condition we desire, then outside forces, including fear, doubt, and the opinions of others, will act upon us.

The second principle is related to the first. This principle is **Increase or Decrease**. The very nature of purposeful action (saving, investing, giving, etc.) leads to increase. Inaction leads to decrease, and eventually outside forces (taxes, interest, inflation, etc.) act upon you and take your money. There was a time in my life when it seemed that no matter how much income I made I would decrease financially. I would receive my customary 2-3% annual raises, but I couldn't seem to stay ahead financially. It wasn't until years later, after a financial crisis in my life, that I realized the importance of increasing.

Always remember that money comes to those who seek to increase. It really doesn't matter if you increase a lot or a little. Money tends to flee those who do nothing with it, as the slothful steward learned in verse 28: "Therefore take the talent from him, and give it to him who has ten talents" (NKJV).

The third principle is **Faithfulness in Little, then Rulership in Much**. The Bible presents this principle in verses 22-23. A strong sense of duty and responsibility are essential for any ruler. This is part of an individual's character and is best observed when dealing with small things (matters). If a matter is entrusted into your hands, it must become important to you, no matter the size. Once you can accept faithfulness in little as your task, then you will be ready for rulership over more. I remember a conversation about money that I had with a member of my church. She told me that she saw nothing wrong with consistently spending a dollar here or there on sodas, chips, etc. I knew right then that she wasn't ready for rulership in her finances. Now, don't get me wrong, I have nothing against goodies, but this woman didn't value a dollar. And if you don't value a dollar when you have a few, then what will your attitude be if you have many dollars? So until she is able to be faithful with one dollar, the likelihood of her being given rulership over many dollars is slim.

Exercises

1. Using the Windows of Stewardship model, assess your Time, Personal, and Financial Stewardship style.

2. Evaluate your Time Stewardship. Ask yourself the following questions:
   What is the monetary value I place on my time?
   What is the personal value I place on my time?
   How well do I manage (spend) my time?
   Do I spend my time developing/searching out my talents?
   Do I give my time to others, abandoning the mission God gave me?

3. Evaluate your Personal Stewardship.
   How do I feel about my talent? Is it valuable?

4. Evaluate your Financial Stewardship. Ask yourself the following questions:
   How do I manage my money?
   Do I have a financial plan?
   Do I have financial goals, or is my spending out of control?
   Am I actively seeking ways to increase my money?
   What are some of those ways?

Summary

Three Principles of True Stewardship
Act or be Acted Upon
Increase or Decrease
Be Faithful in Little, Become Ruler over Much

Time Stewardship
Balance your priorities
Choose your activities,
Develop abilities to skills

Personal Stewardship
Identify your moneymaking talent or ability
Practice your talent once identified

Financial Stewardship
Manage your money
Invest (increase) your money

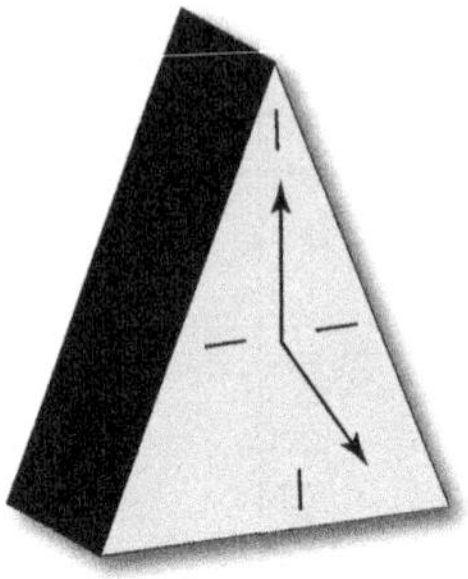

Chapter 2
Time Stewardship

Several years ago while in school I was working on a very important project when I decided to go play basketball with my buddies instead of finishing the project that was due the next day. Knowing the teacher liked me, I decided to ask for more time. To my surprise, she denied my request. I was devastated because my grade suffered from her decision. Little did I realize it at the time, but my grade suffered not from her decision, but from mine. If my project was so important, why didn't I complete the project first and play basketball another day? I thought time was something that could be given, for example, "Give me more time," but I was wrong. In fact, time can be only consumed, and I consumed it unwisely in that situation.

Since time can be only consumed, it would behoove us to consume time efficiently and effectively. This is the essence of time stewardship. Time stewardship is not just time management. Time stewardship involves the use of time consistent with your established mission in life, requiring both a schedule of your time for management and commitment of a certain amount of time to practice for increase and discovering your purpose.

Buried in the hole

Before banks offered deposit insurance, many savers in the deep rural south routinely buried their money in a hole. This common practice was done to protect valuable items from thieves. The parable of the stewards provides different insight into the term "buried in the hole". "So I was afraid and went out and hid your talent in the ground. See, here is what belongs to you" (Matthew 25:25 NIV). In this instance, the term "buried in the hole" is the result of attempting to hide from our responsibilities, opportunities, goals, and dreams. We "bury" these items in a hole through three actions:

1. Failure to Prioritize (Move to Avoid, Not to Achieve)
2. Distractions (Cares of this Life)
3. Misinterpretation of Desired Results (You are a hard man)

Failure to Prioritize (Move to Avoid, Not to Achieve)

As I mentioned earlier in the chapter, instead of completing my project, I decided to play basketball. There was nothing inherently wrong with playing basketball. My mistake involved the failure to prioritize what needed to be done, which led me to move to avoid what was important and not move to achieve what was important. We are always moving in life, moving to avoid a perceived hardship or moving to attain a perceived benefit.

How soon we achieve the goal and avoid negative consequences is affected by our ability and willingness to prioritize. Time stewardship is not possible without the commitment to prioritize. By prioritize, I mean list or rate in order of importance. Lack of prioritization skills keeps us in a state of confusion. Because each alternative is not properly weighed against the others, we are always making a decision based on how we feel at the moment. Having an idea or a schedule already planned out empowers us to use our energies toward the task at hand.

Failure to prioritize can easily lead us to another form of delay, procrastination. By immediately moving and putting their talents to work, the good stewards moved toward achieving their goals, while the wicked, lazy steward moved to avoid loss by burying his talent in a hole.

Distractions (Cares of this Life)

"And take heed to yourselves, lest at any time your hearts be overcharged with surfeiting, and drunkenness, and cares of this life, and so that day come upon you unawares" (Luke 21:34 KJV).

When the master left on his journey, he gave no indication of when he would be returning. The scripture says in Matthew 25:19 that after a long time the master of those servants came to settle accounts with them.

When you are not aware when to expect a visitor, it's proper to make sure that you are prepared with all the necessities for taking care of your visitor. As a result, it was the stewards' responsibility (as it is ours) to be prepared and avoid being snared by the "cares of this life". The wicked lazy steward allowed the cares of this life to prevent him from giving proper attention to the talent given him by the master. The good stewards were those who would not allow distractions to divert their attention from using and increasing the master's talent. The scripture says that they immediately went about their business of increasing the master's talents.

The world we live in is filled with many enjoyable and worthwhile pursuits like education, art, charity, sports, music, entertainment, work, games, etc. At face value these pursuits seem harmless, but we may be overlooking one thing. Once engrossed, we tend to leave God and/or His purpose for our lives on the outside. We must learn to control distractions.

Control distractions by beginning a task with the expected end in mind. Possess a clear picture of the goal or destination before you actually start. Beginning with the end in mind helps you understand where you are now, envision where you want to be, and ensure that the steps you are taking are in the direction of your goals.

It's obvious that the good stewards had a clear picture of the end in the beginning, because they immediately went about making that picture come to pass. In contrast, the bad steward didn't have a clear picture at all, because he did nothing, not even the minimum response of depositing the talent with the bankers.

Based on the principle of beginning with the end in mind, there are two creations: a mental creation, and a physical creation. Without a mental creation we fail to balance our priorities properly. They shift based on what is happening on the outside in the (physical world). To manage your time properly, begin in the mental world (the world you create). I will present more on the mental world in chapter 3.

The world system competes with your priorities on a moment, by, moment basis. From food to games, television, movies, music -- the list of things is endless. As we lose the battle, we find that we don't have time for the things we say we want to accomplish: learning a new language, going back to school, writing a book, volunteering, etc. Those things which we say are dear to our hearts are the things that we don't do. To regain a foothold on time, we must retreat to the mental world and begin to create what we want while establishing a timetable for completing the things we say we want to accomplish.

Misinterpetation of Desired Results (You are a hard man)

Opportunities are all around us. Life has taught me that the successful people and the unsuccessful people of the world view their opportunities completely differently. Successful people view their opportunities as a means for achieving their goals and making their dreams and desires come true. Unsuccessful people tend to view the opportunities as threats of failure, harm, or embarrassment. That successful people have a positive view of their opportunities doesn't mean that all of their plans work out the first time or they are more successful than anyone else. They realize, however, that as they take advantage of all the opportunities that are in line with their goals, the willingness to consistently move toward opportunities increases their ability to maximize results.

In the parable of the stewards, the lazy steward saw his opportunity as being potentially harmful (the master was a hard man), and as a result he felt safer hiding his talent to keep from losing it. How do you view your talents? Do you see your opportunity to shine as an opportunity to be embarrassed? The lazy steward's response (you are a hard man) gives us insight into his misinterpretation of the master's desired results.

God is not against us, He is for us. Those who trust in Him for salvation believe He corrects us and seeks to lead us into the Kingdom of God. Having intimate knowledge of our sinful nature, we know that we should be punished for our actions and fear that He is out to get us.

Although God hates sin, He loves the sinner and is merciful by raining His blessings “on the just and on the unjust” (Matthew 5:45 KJV). If that were not the case, He would not have given each of us unique talents to bless us and allow us to be a blessing to others. Because He is for us (Romans 8:31), He has set Himself free to bless us (Philippians 4:19). Knowing that we are completely forgiven releases us from feeling that we don’t have what it takes to please God.

Dig up your Treasure by Discovering your Purpose

The world system teaches us to bury our treasure, but God would have us dig up our treasure (talents) and share them with others. The words of my mentor, Bishop Henry Porter, ring true in my ears: “To prosper in life we must come to realize that the highest and best use for our lives is God’s purpose for our creation.” Everything else in our lives revolves around that purpose.

“Purpose” is an interesting word. Merriam-Webster’s Dictionary defines purpose as something set up as an object or end to be attained. Defining purpose is easy, but maintaining purpose is a little more challenging. Your life’s purpose is being assaulted daily by your desires, the desires of others, distractions, etc. I developed an acronym to highlight what I believe is needed to maintain your purpose:

PURPOSE-ACRONYM

PASSION - The object of your enthusiasm

UNDERSTANDING - Perceiving and comprehending the nature and significance of; getting the idea

REALIZATION - Understanding something clearly and distinctly

PERSISTENCE - Persevering; continuing or repeating behavior

OUTSTANDING - Still existing; needing to be settled or resolved

SPECIFIC - Particularly fitting a use or purpose; special, distinctive, or unique

EXCELLENCE - Doing well

Goals

Once you arrive at your purpose, goal setting is a must. A goal is your guide through a clear understanding of your destination. Goals keep you going when times get rough. People tend to think that goals are best written down and packed away until the beginning of the new year, when you promise to adhere to last year's resolution. But they are so much more: a goal is what separates you from the masses, from those who live life according to the wishes of others. They are swept along by the currents of mediocrity. In contrast, a goal-oriented person has resolved within himself to take life by the horns and shape his destiny according to his purpose and objectives.

Goals are a reminder of your commitment to yourself to complete/ achieve your purpose and desires. By setting goals based on your main purpose first, and other objectives, you set the tone for selecting tasks that are consistent with your purpose and wishes. Goals are an extremely important component of time management. They ensure that you are doing more than just completing tasks, that you are completing tasks that further your purpose.

Control your Distractions

Purposeful goals help control distractions through a plan. We live in a world filled with many wonderful distractions, and they are needed. Our bodies aren't designed solely for work. God in His infinite wisdom designed our bodies with many pleasure receptors to enjoy His creation. The problem arises when we allow distractions to become the enemies of our goals, and not a means to an end.

Planning for distractions is comparable to traveling on a long road trip and viewing the sights during the journey. You take time to see the sights along the way. Being distracted is comparable to stopping to sightsee with no regard for when you arrive at your destination. You're just standing still, not taking action toward goal fulfillment.

Task Management

Paying bills, going to work, cooking dinner, picking up the dry cleaning, volunteering, etc. – our lives are filled with a myriad of tasks that need to be completed on an ongoing basis. The need for the completion of these tasks solidifies the necessity for time management. Time management is essential for using your time to complete the maximum amount of your daily, weekly, and monthly tasks. Due to the hectic nature of present day life, it can be quite easy to be overwhelmed by the sheer volume of tasks we feel we need to complete.

The basics of time management teach us to select the four main categories in which we spend time: emotional, physical, spiritual, and vocational. Listed below are examples of a few sub-categories for each of the four main time categories:

Physical: Sleep, Sex, Exercise, Eating
Emotional: Reading, Entertainment, Socializing with Friends
Spiritual: Prayer, Bible Reading, Volunteering, Public Worship

Vocational: Job, Business, Projects

Using 168 hours per week, allocate your time based on your goals and objectives in the four main categories. Next, record your tasks in a systematic order for prioritization and completion. This is done by assigning letter a, b, or c to each task, with "a" being the most urgent and "c" being the least urgent.

Here's an example:

Complete financial report
Volunteer at charity
Cook dinner

In order of priority and importance we may categorize the tasks in the following manner:

A Complete the financial report - vocational

B Cook dinner – physical

C Volunteer at charity - spiritual

The next step of time management requires you to assign a date and time when you will address the task at hand and record it on your planner sheet.

Here's an example:

	Monday	Tuesday	Wednesday	Thursday	Friday
8:00 am	Financial Report				
9:00 am	Cook Breakfast		Volunteer at Charity		

A Complete the financial report

B Cook breakfast

C Volunteer at charity

Finally, at the end of the week review the weekly planner, and carry forward to a defined future period any items that were not completed but need to be completed. Using the example from above, something else that was more important came up, and you were unable to volunteer at charity this week, so move it to your next week's planner list.

	Monday	Tuesday	Wednesday	Thursday	Friday
8:00 pm	Volunteer at Charity	Cook Dinner			
9:00 pm	Review Report				

A Review report

B Cook dinner

C Volunteer at charity

Time Increase

Our lives consist of more than completing tasks. We have a responsibility to improve our talent on a consistent basis. The Japanese call this Kaizen, a philosophy of continual improvement. The goal of Kaizen Philosophy is to involve a measure of our time implementing small improvement ideas (practice) on a regular basis. The end result is increased proficiency in what you do. Devoting a portion of time for increase is the material for creating.

For example, it's been said that opportunities are created by those who are best prepared. Practice is also the means by which your abilities are developed into skills. The Parable of the Talents teaches us that the good stewards used the time between the master's departure and his return to develop their innate abilities into skills which led to an increase in their talents.

Unlike the good stewards, the lazy steward didn't use the time available to develop his ability into a skill. He didn't respect the relationship between time and skill development. Skills are developed, over time, by repetition. Because the lazy steward didn't use his time to develop his ability, the master, upon his return, took the talent away from the lazy-servant, leaving him with the ability, but not the means, for developing a skill.

I talk with many people who have incredible abilities, but they have chosen not to use their time to develop skills. They go through life saying things like, "I wished I would have furthered my education when I had the chance," or "I was always good with numbers, I should have become an accountant." Skillful people, because of their preparedness, reap the benefits. The more you miss opportunities, fewer opportunities seem to come your way.

Time's Dual Purpose

Time serves a dual purpose. On the one hand, proper time management enables us to accomplish tasks on a daily basis. On the other hand, intentional time investment serves as a means to develop ourselves. Traveling offers an example of time management and increase and their relationship and importance to each other. If you are traveling to a far-off place, time management will ensure that you are using your hours efficiently, while time increase will ensure that you are traveling in the right direction. Each operates independently, but they compliment each other. Without time management you would be traveling in the right direction but have no idea of when you would be arriving. Without time increase you would travel efficiently but have no idea where you are going.

Chapter 3
Personal Stewardship Finances

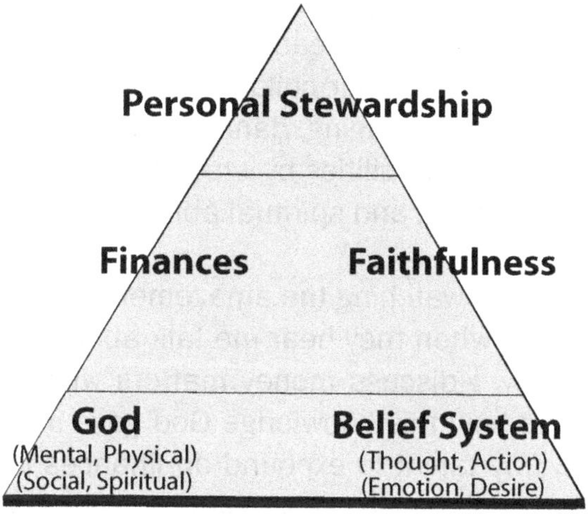

To be good stewards we must be given something over which to be stewards. God provides us access to assets that cause us to increase financially. What is an asset? An asset is anything of economic value, controlled by an individual or business, that can be converted to cash. Finances are given to us through our abilities/talents (assets). Our abilities determine how much in finances we receive. Matthew 25:14-15 illustrates this truth.

v14 "Again, it will be like a man going on a journey, who called his servants and entrusted his property to them.
v15 To one he gave five talents of money, to another two talents, and to another one talent, each according to his ability" (NIV).

Discern Your Assets

God is a God of increase. And because He is such, He expects us to manage and increase the money He entrusts to us. In this parable, God is portrayed as the master. The master gave his servants money according to their ability to manage and increase. The servants were the stewards. It was their job to manage and increase the money of the master. This parable is applicable in each one of our lives. God has given each of us abilities that, if applied correctly, will not only provide for us, but increase His Kingdom as well. We each possess a latent gift, something we usually begin to exhibit in our childhood. We basically develop an ability, whether its painting, singing, dancing, reading, talking, praying, etc. There are four areas of abilities by which finances come to us. They are mental, physical, social, and spiritual abilities.

Mental Abilities I enjoy watching the amazement-filled faces of participants in my seminars when they hear me talk about personal finances in a truly unique way. I discuss money matters with such confidence and knowledge, and how this knowledge God gave me has helped me prosper financially. My talent to expound on finances is an example of a mental asset. In the financial arena mental assets are simply mental abilities/talents from God, which enable you to increase financially through the creation of new ideas, solving of problems, and provision of knowledge beneficial to others. Mental assets are successfully developed by what you read, study, and hear. Those with mental assets should exercise extreme caution in what they look at and listen to, and how they attend to it. I believe that people possessing mental assets are very receptive to their environment. Therefore, these stewards should strive to dwell consistently in environments suitable for developing their gift. The effect of excessive distractions on the mind has been well documented. Both the quantity and the content of distractions contribute to the underdevelopment of mental assets in most people.

Each of us has mental assets: some of us are good with numbers, while some are good with words. Some have used mental assets to become teachers, lawyers, doctors, business owners, etc., in order to earn money. Examples of people possessing mental assets include:

a)Bill Gates, who used his mental abilities to create Windows® computer software. As a result of using his mental abilities, Mr. Gates has become the world's wealthiest man.

b)Alexander Graham Bell, who used his mental abilities to invent the telephone, an essential tool in our lives today.

c)Thomas Edison, whose invention of the light bulb through use of his mental abilities was revolutionary. The invention of the light bulb sparked the utilization of electric power.

Physical Abilities When I was in high school my buddies and I gathered around a television to watch the NBA slam-dunk contest. Michael Jordan won the competition that year with a dunk from the free throw line. The prize money amounted to more than $10,000 dollars!!! Jordan, using a single facet of his myriad of physical assets, garnered money and increased financially. Physical assets are God-given abilities/talents that enable you to prosper financially using your physical body to create things, solve problems, and perform tasks in a completely unique way. Those possessing physical assets develop their skills by practice and repetition. Stewards possessing physical assets suffer when they don't practice consistently. Inconsistent practice doesn't provide enough time to develop physical assets properly.

Although many of us are unable to leap and dunk from the free-throw line, there are several other physical assets, such as painting, sculpture, singing, playing an instrument, etc., which can also provide finances. In each area of physical talent, we must remember that our talent is unique and should not be compared with others. What if Yolanda Adams had decided not to become a gospel singer because she didn't sound like Mahalia Jackson? The world would have missed the blessing of her incredible gift. The gift would have remained as buried treasure.

Mind and Body Connection I subscribe to the school of thought that the mind and body are one. Whatever affects one affects the other. Whether positively or negatively, your mental and physical assets respond to what happens to the body and mind respectively, in turn affecting your level of success. One personal example, eating foods that don't provide sufficient nutrition for the body limits your mental level of performance. I learned this the hard way while working on this book. During that time I was eating foods that didn't contribute to a healthy body. I also stopped exercising. Over a period of time, I grew lethargic, and it became increasingly difficult to concentrate. My level of knowledge didn't change, the fuel feeding my body did. As a result, my mental asset responded accordingly. I compare this to running an expensive high performance foreign car on the lowest octane gasoline. Running the car on the lowest octane didn't change the fact that the car was a high performance automobile, it only impaired the results.

Practice Earlier in this chapter I referred to one of the greatest basketball players, Michael Jordan. In his hey day, Michael Jordan possessed remarkable physical abilities. There were other basketball players who were physically gifted as well as or better than he was. But I believe what separated him from all the rest was his understanding of how much better he could perform based on the belief he established in his mind. He believed that practice would make him the greatest player ever, and his belief prompted him to practice. He demonstrated that consistent practice leads to high degrees of success. I remember an article in which Jordan, describing his contemporaries, said that he knew that he was better than they were when he saw how lax they were in practice. He knew that pure talent could take them only so far. Practice separates the high achiever from the mediocre one.

Social Abilities Your friends can make you or break you. Social assets include the abilities to make friends and to establish relationships with people of influence. People possessing social assets have learned to put themselves in social environments to meet people who can help them accomplish God's mission for their lives. They also realize that their social associations can have a positive or negative outcome. As a result, they have developed an uncommon ability to put maximum effort into their relationships, because the amount of effort they put into the relationship affects the level of blessing that comes out. Through social relationships God delivers finances and opportunities for you to fulfill your mission or purpose.

It was David's social relationship with Jonathan that began to elevate his status within King Saul's palace (1 Samuel 18:1, 3; 19:7). Jonathan gave David royal clothes (1 Samuel 18:4) and inside information which was crucial in David's survival and eventual ascension to the throne (1 Samuel 20:35-42; 23:16-18). As king, David provided for Jonathan's son (2 Samuel 9).

Elisha and the Shunammite woman (2 Kings 4:8-37; 8:1-6) also illustrate the blessing of a social relationship. The Shunammite woman insisted that Elisha eat some food at her home while traveling through her town. After the initial dinner, she would invite Elisha to dinner at her home whenever he passed through town. Later, in conversation with her husband, she says that she knows that Elisha is a holy man of God (man of influence). Please note that she never asked anything of Elisha during this period of time, she only extended her kindness. Over time, this kindness included establishing a small upper room furnished with a bed, table, chair, and lamp for Elisha's use whenever needed. Eventually, Elisha wanted to repay her for her kindness, but she said she neither needed nor desired anything. Elisha's servant, Gehazi, noticed that she had no children. Then Elisha blessed her to conceive a child with her husband who was old. One day, the child became ill and died. The Shunammite woman took the child to Elisha's room and went to get the man of God. Elisha raised the boy from the dead and healed him of his illness.

Because she had established a relationship with Elisha through the use of her social abilities, the Shunammite woman was made aware by Elisha of the impending famine, and was given instructions by him on how to survive and thrive during this seven-year famine. The Bible doesn't indicate that Elisha spoke this word to anyone else; it tells us of the Shunammite woman.

Several of you may have been empowered for the mission God wants you to do by this ability to attract material support from people God wants to help you and/or finance the mission. You have discovered that you don't need to postpone your mission because of lack of your own funds. Your relationships or favor with people bring to you what you need.

Spiritual Abilities Prayer changes things. Prayer changes the effects of your past, impacts the events of your present, and empowers and constructs your future. If you don't believe me, then read the autobiography of Conrad Hilton, ***Be My Guest***.

In his autobiography Mr. Hilton spoke of how he attended 6:00 am prayer daily to work things out in his favor financially. He discovered that the spiritual realm contains material for the physical realm. Therefore he concluded that spiritual actions (prayer) could impact the very financial need he had in his life at that moment. Certainly there are some who would say that it was luck or business savvy on his part, but Mr. Hilton didn't stop attending prayer, and his hotel chain is now known worldwide.

Spiritual assets are the ability to benefit financially through our relationship with and service to God. Faithfulness to God is an asset because God causes you to increase. His presence and His principles cause this. Take note of the biblical story in which Jesus instructed Peter to go fishing for money to pay their taxes and the money appeared in the fish's mouth. That was nothing short of a miracle, and that miracle would not have occurred had it not been for the spiritual asset Jesus had in his obedient relationship to God the Father.

God blesses you through any one or combination of these assets, as in the case of the widow's oil and Elisha (2 Kings 4:3-5).

a) Elisha the prophet told her to borrow jars from her neighbors to put oil in. Had she not developed her social assets or possessed social assets, perhaps her neighbors would not have given her the jars.
b) The widow's husband possessed a spiritual asset in his relationship

with God, even after death!! The scriptures say that he revered the Lord (2 Kings 4:1). Because of this relationship, I believe, God supernaturally assisted in the provision for his survivors.

Those who love God and spend time with Him develop something. Each relationship with another individual can bring out your best or worst characteristics. As you spend time with God, whatever gift, talent, or ability is inside of you is brought out, because a relationship with Him does that – it adds to you.

Service to God through ministry to others will cause them in turn to minister to you financially. Several of God's servants benefited because of this principle (Romans 15:26-27):

v26 For Macedonia and Achaia were pleased to make a contribution for the poor among the saints in Jerusalem.
v27 They were pleased to do it, and indeed they owe it to them. For if the Gentiles have shared in the Jews' spiritual blessings, they owe it to the Jews to share with them their material blessings (NIV).

Abraham was a friend of God (2 Chronicles 20:7). His friendship with God enabled him to become wealthy and a Father of Nations (Genesis 17:5).

Discover Your Talent

Identifying our talents is a difficult task for some and an easy one for others. I believe that when we tune our hearts, we'll intercept the signal identifying our talents, and we'll receive directions. Three means for tuning our hearts are inquire of God, learn through suffering, and ask yourself questions.

1. Inquire of God Matthew 7:7-8 "Ask, and it will be given to you, seek, and you will find; knock and the door will be opened for you. For everyone who asks receives; he who seeks finds; and to him who knocks, the door will be opened" (NIV). Put in plain terms, God wants us to fulfill His purpose for our creation. He is willing to share intimate knowledge of ourselves with us to provide guidance. Years ago, after arriving in a new city, I was unsure about what career I should pursue. I possessed a degree in Business Administration, but my past experience in business had proved to be unsuccessful, and I felt uncomfortable re-entering the business arena. I inquired of God, and He told me through my pastor that my talent was managing and that I was a manager. God told me in no uncertain terms that regardless of my past lack of success in business, I was a manager. Without hesitation, I sought employment in a managerial position. Within two weeks, I was hired as an Accounts Receivable Manager and subsequently promoted one year later to Chief Financial Officer.

2. Learn through suffering Earlier this year, I met a woman who shared a testimony of how through her pain and anguish God commissioned her to write a book telling her story through poetry. Prior to her suffering she had no inkling of the greatness that was inside her and the purpose for which she was created. She wasn't created to suffer, but suffering put her in a position to open herself to her true purpose. Her testimony reminds me of Joseph's suffering in the Egyptian prison. He was sold into slavery by his brothers, falsely accused of rape, and thrown into prison. All of this seemed to be because of his brothers, but listen to what he said to them when they were in his presence more than 15 years later: "Now therefore, be not grieved, nor angry with yourselves, that ye sold me hither: for God did send me before you to preserve life" (Genesis 45:5 KJV). That may explain why many of us don't receive direction until we go through something. When we go through something we cry out to God and He answers.

3. Ask yourself questions Two years after my promotion to Chief Financial Officer, God told me to do business in deep waters, venture into an area of my field beyond my present experience. That sounded like an intriguing idea, but my problem was I didn't know what to do. Finally, after spending time trying to decide what I wanted to do, I began to wake up in the middle of the night, because the lack of an answer disturbed me. One night in particular, I sat in my bedroom and asked myself this question: What is the one sentence that captures my mission in life? So I sat there for hours in the quiet, alone with my thoughts, opening my mind and heart completely to determine what gives me the most fulfillment, and I arrived at this statement: My mission is to lead a blessed and prosperous life and to teach others how to do the same. That one sentence captured the essence of what I am and what I was to do. It incorporated what God told me years ago concerning management, in addition to other things He didn't tell me at that time, because I needed training to understand the vision and overcome my fears. Your talent is probably the one that your fears seek to prevent you from embracing. What is it that you do, but are afraid to do? This is what you were created to do. Listen to the inner voice; it is the outer voices that are made of the world system and the opinions of others that you hear when you back away from who you are. We adopt mental blocks that literally lock us into a self-depreciating mode of thinking. We have been taught to value the voices that tell us who we are and what we can't do. We must begin to listen to the voice that says we can. The scriptures say that the enemy of our souls is a roaring lion (1 Peter 5:8). Don't let the roar immobilize you, causing you to forget who you are. How can you be free? Address the fears in your mind head on. Listen to who God says that you are. God delights in telling us who we are. The enemy tries to use our surroundings, failures, and comparisons with others to define us.

Don't compare yourself to others We know too much about ourselves. Gideon was one who knew too much about himself. He said that he was the least in his tribe which was the least in all of Israel. Stewards who have difficulty discovering their talents allow what they see in comparison with others to define who they are. God is the one who defines who you are. In Saul's ascension to the throne of Israel we see how God operated in the life of a person who defined himself by the words and opinions of others. In 1 Samuel 9:21, Saul says that he is a Benjamite, the smallest tribe in Israel, and that his family is the least of the families of Benjamin, but God had said (1 Samuel 9:17) that he was to be king.

Forget your failure(s); focus on your many successes Moses knew that he was the deliverer for the Israelites, but when he tried to help them, they responded negatively to him, prompting him to run away from the gift for 40 years. The voices of others can cause you to see yourself incorrectly. Eventually Moses became content to live with the man who became his father-in-law (Exodus 2:21). Acts 7:22 KJV reads, "Moses was learned in all the wisdom of the Egyptians, and was mighty in words and in deeds." Despite his talents and gifts, Moses' focus on failure immobilized him for 40 years.

After I answered my question about my mission in life, my thoughts were attuned to answering these subsequent questions specifically and precisely:

a) What would I do if money or lack of money were no concern?
b) What gives me joy?
c) Where do I see myself in five years? Ten years?
d) Where do my greatest assets lie: physical, mental, spiritual and social?
e) How could I incorporate those assets into my mission?

Those are some of the questions I used to clarify my thinking. As a result, my talent has evolved from securing employment in management to starting a company providing financial management and writing a book on Stewardship.

Develop Your Talent

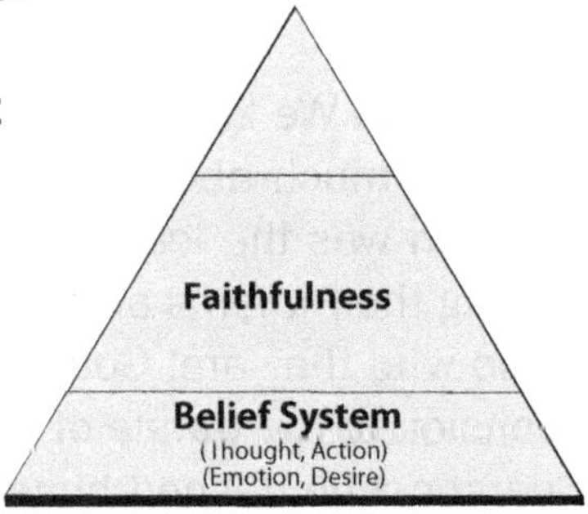

Personal Stewardship - Financial Faithfulness Your faithfulness comes from your belief systems. In the parable of Stewardship, the lazy steward highlights the effect of a poor belief system and how its components interact with each other. It was his thoughts about the master that caused him to experience the emotion of fear. This emotional experience created a desire within himself to return what the master had given him. This desire resulted in his action of hiding the talent in the ground. Negative thoughts are the seeds of the diabolical adversary, the devil. The devil tries to manipulate the components of your belief system to delay and distract you. His intentions are to steal your belief in your gift or ability. He seeks to accomplish this by bombarding your mind with thoughts of fear, doubt, and discouragement. Satan realizes that thoughts either stretch you or contract you, so whenever an opportunity for advancement arises, he presents you with "reality," i.e., he highlights your limitations to cause you to shrink away from your opportunity. If he is successful in stealing your belief that your ability can earn money, then the ability begins to fade away from lack of practice, and opportunity to earn money from your abilities fades away, reinforcing the belief that your ability is worthless. Your belief system is comprised of the following components: thoughts, emotions, desire, and actions.

Thoughts Once your financial destination is firmly embedded in your thoughts, it will become reality. This is due to the universal/mental law. This particular law dictates that whatever is persistently in your mental life manifests itself materially. The name of this law is, "As he thinketh in his heart, so is he" (Proverbs 23:7, KJV). This scripture is the sum of several laws:

a) <u>One must use or one will lose</u>. In the parable of the good steward, the lazy, unfruitful steward was given a talent that he might use the means at his disposal to manage and increase. This steward chose, however, not to use the talent, but instead to hide it in the ground. The master, upon returning, expected to see an increase but did not. The talent was then taken from the unprofitable servant because he didn't use it, and the talent was given to the profitable servant, because he did use what was given to him.

b) <u>Believe it and you shall have it</u>. The unprofitable servant believed the master to be harsh and cruel. He believed that the master reaped where he didn't sow. His belief system was not one that led to financial increase. Belief leads to faith, which leads to financial increase, miracles, etc. Jesus asked the two blind men if they believed he could heal them (Matthew 9:28). When people didn't believe, Jesus didn't do many miracles (Matthew 3:58).

c) Thoughts create reality. The unprofitable steward thought that his lord was a cruel man. As a result of his thoughts, his actions created a situation where this thought came to pass. Whether you believe in the enemy of confidence or not, realize that there is an opposing force that seeks to prevent you from excelling through the talents given to you by God. We may not readily know who the enemy of confidence is, but we feel his efforts through lack of confidence, discouragement, and low self-esteem. Many of you are unaware of his tactics. He introduces these negative thoughts you believe originated from your mind. You don't recognize they were induced by an enemy who delights in keeping you from being the great person that God announced to the world through your gifts and talents. Your talents serve as evidence of God's pronouncement of your greatness. Through deception, the enemy seeks to use our great power against us. He is very familiar with the universal laws ordained by God, particularly, "As he thinketh in his heart, so is he." Your thoughts about yourself can lead you down one of two paths. The path you were born to travel leads to the successful use of, belief in, and realization of your goals, objectives, and dreams. The alternate path leads to lack of use, doubt concerning, and failure to achieve your goals and dreams. Therefore, when your thoughts (induced or other wise) are persistent in your mind, then those are the results. Thoughts which bring depression, discouragement, and doubt lead to the second path.

Unfortunately, most of us are not born rich. We have to rise from less than ideal situations and circumstances to achieve riches. So how can that be done when we don't think we can prosper like the rich man? The Word of God is the answer. Deuteronomy 8:3, quoted in Matthew 4:4 and Luke 4:4, says men shall not live by bread alone, but by every word of God. The Word of God gives you life. As you digest God's Word, that Word in turn becomes a part of you. Simply put, the more positive, inspirational, and motivational words that you can access mentally, the greater the likelihood that you will be able to identify and ignore the words which lead to discouragement, etc. Always remember that the words you write or speak are but an extension of the thoughts you allowed to roam freely in your mind, forming your thinking patterns. More often than not, these patterns were established with the opinions of others that are not conducive to successful implementation of your goals.

Before we were saved we had thoughts about ourselves that we would never be wealthy or great. Well, God wants us to realize that belief in Jesus saves us, but it's the Word which remakes us. The Word of God de-programs and re-programs us into believing that we deserve and can acquire wealth now. The Word puts everyone on a level playing field. The person who is in debt, the person who is afraid, the person who has doubt -- they all can have their thoughts re-programmed by the Word. Riches become accessible to them, just like riches are accessible to highly talented and gifted people. Why? Because the Word causes you to believe in your talents. Your talents can and will bring wealth to you, but you must believe they can before the riches come.

Your thoughts form the foundation of wherever you currently are financially. If you have $5.00 thoughts then you will have $5.00 money. If you think there is no way out of your situation, then your mind will create that type of situation for you. Every experience you created in life had its origins in your mind. The amounts of money you earn, possess, owe, and spend are based on your thinking patterns about money. Think about it. What are your thoughts about money?

a) Is your first thought to spend it, or save it?
b) When you think of credit, do you use it for purchasing consumer goods you normally couldn't afford, or for investing in stocks or real estate?
c) Do you believe that you can earn more, or that have you reached your maximum earnings potential?
d) Is money, or the love of money the root of all evil? (See 1 Timothy 6:10, KJV.)

Your answers to these and similar questions will reveal your thoughts about money. Are your answers limiting you to poverty, or guiding you to riches? Possessing more money is not the answer to poverty. The amount of money is irrelevant, because the same thought pattern is influencing what you do with the money. If you have a poverty consciousness, you may feel that whenever you want something you should get it, even if it means using credit cards to buy it. By purchasing this item using credit you are spending more than the money you have available, thereby creating debt.

You have a poverty thought pattern when you create debt that takes money out of your hands instead of incurring debt that brings money into your hands. For example, by purchasing clothes on credit you are creating debt that takes money out of your pockets via monthly credit card payments with no monetary return. On the other hand, buying a house on credit and renting it to a tenant is using debt in a way that brings money to you. That's an example of how you would use debt, if you possessed a rich person's thought patterns. Many of you are probably asking,

a) What causes people to think that way?
b) Why does it seem so difficult to think prosperously?
c) How are people who are born in poverty able to rise above their situation to acquire great riches?

Mental programming is the answer.

Mental Programming As I mentioned earlier, the Word of God de-programs and re-programs your mind for prosperity. Use of affirmations will also help greatly in accomplishing this task. I define affirmations as statements made in present tense describing the way you want the future to look in your life. The Word of God and affirmations de-program the negative/incorrect mental programming we have received over the course of our lives. Whether we are aware of it or not, our thoughts are a result of prior programming. We were not born with the thoughts we have now, they were formed as a result of the programming we received. By programming I mean the opinions or comments of other people around us: the things we read, hear, speak, experience, or have been told about ourselves that we come to believe are true.

In my life I've encountered people who planted seeds of positive mental programming in my mind, and the fruit is manifesting itself in my adult life today. My grandmother and mother, in particular, have always been a source of positive inspiration. Whenever I attempted something new, they told me that I could accomplish whatever I set my mind to and that they believed in me. I believed them, and whenever I attempt something new, to this day, I hear their voices saying, "We believe in you." That's the thought I have. I believe that anything is possible for me if I put my all into it.

How's that for positive programming? That seemingly minute programming affected my thought life in childhood and beyond. It's the driving force behind all my successful endeavors. Conversely, negative programming has the opposite result. There are people who are talented, beautiful, witty, intelligent, and gifted, but were programmed otherwise, creating a belief that they lack the very thing they already have. How many of you have heard about young girls literally starving themselves to death because they received (and believed) negative programming indicating they were fat? Do these statements sound familiar to anyone?

a) You will never amount to anything in life.
b) You are clumsy.
c) You talk too much.
d) You don't talk enough.
e) You are shy.
f) You are not as smart as your brother is.
g) Your sister has the looks, while you have the brains.
h) You are ugly.

These negative statements and many others like them are heard by millions of children daily. They hear nothing else. This negative programming becomes part of their thinking and eventually manifests itself in their lives now or later in adulthood.

Are you wondering why you don't earn the money you want, or why you have not achieved the goals you desire? Examine your programming. Somewhere along the line you have heard and accepted programming like this:

a) Money is the root of all evil.
b) Earn enough to be comfortable.
c) Being rich is a hassle.
d) The rich can't sleep for worrying about their money.
e) It's too hard to run a business.
f) You were never good handling money.
g) Money doesn't buy you happiness.
h) Don't try anything new, because you might fail.
i) Failure is bad.
j) You have bad luck.

These seemingly innocent statements and those like them help to form negative/incorrect thinking patterns. These thinking patterns are rehearsed in your brain, becoming so entrenched that in many people these patterns feel such a common part of their lives that they aren't aware of the patterns holding them back from what they want. Once a thinking pattern is developed, it is difficult to change. Why? Because it is a pattern, and we are creatures of habit. Once we have established a pattern of doing something, it feels natural, even comfortable. It seems that we've always been that way and that we can't change. But you can change!! How? By learning how the brain works.

Your brain is not very discerning by nature. It accepts what you program it with, as a computer does, and provides results based on what is entered. I'm sure that those of you who work with computers are familiar with the term GIGO, Garbage In Garbage Out. Simply put, this means if you input garbage into your brain, then you receive garbage out. So, to change the output you must change the input. The first step would be to remove all the negative thoughts and programming you have in your mind now.

I once possessed a fear of public speaking. After an embarrassing speaking situation in college in which I forgot what I wanted to say onstage, I feared that in any future public speaking situations I would not know what to say. I was very depressed. I rehearsed the entire sorry scene in my mind off and on for years. As I'm sure you have guessed by now, in situations following that incident, once onstage I would be so frightened and self-conscious that I would forget some of the things I wanted to say. So, to overcome that forgetting, I had to take the initiative to reprogram my mind, to adjust my thinking pattern. Contrary to what you may think, changing your thinking involves more than consciously thinking differently. It involves de-programming existing mental programs. I began to de-program myself by saying to myself daily:

a) I do not fear public speaking.
b) I no longer forget what I have to say once on stage.
c) I am a successful, effective, and sought-after public speaker.
d) I enjoy public speaking.
e) I thoroughly prepare for my speaking engagements. "Who has made man's mouth? Or who makes the mute, the deaf, the seeing, or the blind? Have not I, the Lord? Now therefore, go, and I will be with your mouth and teach you what you shall say" (Exodus 4:11-12, NKJV).

I recorded these and similar thoughts on tape and began to listen to them persistently and consistently every day. The first two sentences replaced the negative programming with the programming I needed to change my existing thinking pattern. The next three sentences provided my brain a model to follow. The Word of God re-programs my mind even beyond that which affirmations (my human resources) can accomplish in creating the type of thinking pattern I want. My mind fought this at first, telling me that I was wasting my time and that maybe this would work for others, but it wouldn't work for me. Based on the previous negative programming, my mind was thoroughly convinced that I would forever be a failure as a public speaker. After a period of time, this new programming began to work and I began to change. I summoned enough courage to join Toastmasters, an organization which helps people develop public speaking skills and overcome any fears they may have. As a result, I began to overcome the past negative programming and grow in my skill as a public speaker.

This concept may be so foreign to some of you that you don't believe it will work for you. Please believe me, it will. I've read many self-improvement books that suggest that improvement stems from changing your thinking pattern. This is good advice. My concern is that people would think that changing your thinking pattern is as easy as thinking a happy thought!!

Changing your thinking pattern starts with programming. Here's a diagram illustrating how it works:

#1 Change Mental Programming-->Change Thoughts-->New Thinking Patterns
When people are exhorted to change their thinking patterns, they usually approach it in this manner:

#2 Change Thoughts----->New Thinking Patterns
Example #2 is contrary to the way the brain works. Using example #2 will work only as long as you are consciously making an effort to change your thoughts. Changing your thinking pattern through changing mental programming uses the way the brain actually works, empowering permanent change without continual conscious effort.

The importance of focused positive mental programming is highlighted now, because without positive mental programming, your old thoughts will influence your desired new actions with old action, causing you to stop your plan for self-improvement.

Imagination Imagination defined: "n. 1. The action of imagining, or of forming mental images or concepts of what is not actually present to the senses."

Imagination is a God-given ability that enables humanity to create things like God does. Our thoughts are a link to the spiritual realm. Imagination is the creative process by which the mental images from the spiritual realm form material in the natural realm. In comparison, imagination can be viewed as paint and canvas. These items provide a means of expression for the artist. Imagination serves the same purpose for our thoughts and ideas. It is a power that can't be stopped. Once started, eventually, that which is imagined will be accomplished. So, if your thoughts are on becoming prosperous and you begin to imagine wealth in your life, you are in essence pulling the material from the spiritual realm, which will create your wealth in the natural realm. So, consistent imagination is an essential component in advancing to the next level in wealth accumulation, or in any endeavor, for that matter.

While writing this book I suffered from lack of imagination during a period when I needed it the most. I didn't notice it at first, because the desire to accomplish my goal was on the forefront of my mind. But as time passed I encountered growing periods of discouragement and lack of inspiration. It became so great that I could no longer see myself achieving my goals. So I prayed, and this is what I felt the Lord say to my spirit:
"Excessive television is hindering your ability to imagine. It presents imagery that replaces the images you would have received from your imagination. Excessive television also influences you not to imagine, because the images are presented to you. Due to lack of use, your imagination no longer provided power to you from the spiritual realm. So, your power to achieve your goals was limited to the images being force fed into your mind. Thus, any God-inspired thoughts you had could not receive the correct power from those images and were subsequently discounted. It was this lack of power that prevented you from seeing yourself achieve and desire to accomplish your goals. The desires (God-given) didn't match the images presented to your mind. Remember what I said concerning the builders of The Tower of Babel: 'Behold, the people is one, and they have all one language; and this they begin to do: and now nothing will be restrained from them, which they have imagined to do' [Genesis 11:6, KJV]. And, since you no longer imagined but began to function on the images presented, you became subject to the limitations of those images."

I wasn't aware at the time that the longer you watch television, the more likely you will be put into a trance-like state called alpha mode. Alpha is when your mind is in a non-cognitive, passive, receptive mode. The mind slips into alpha mode while watching television due to the lack of eye movement while watching television. Because most television screens are relatively small, very little eye movement is required to absorb all of the images on the screen. There is a direct correlation between eye movement and thought stimulation. While one's mind is in alpha mode, it is being taken advantage of by Advertisers who are using the mind's receptive mode to instill in the viewer a desire for their product. During the time I began writing this book, I was experiencing increased stress from my job. The stress began to sap my energy. So when I arrived at home I would plop down in front of the television to relax. After watching a couple of shows, I would try to write, but nothing significant would happen. So I would go to bed. This pattern repeated itself for months. Not only was I not writing anything significant, but also I was growing increasingly tired after each day as I tried to work on this book.

With my imagination being limited, my focus was on reality, limiting myself to what had already happened in my life (past) and what I could see happening based on current circumstances (present). There was no thought for the future, only what happened before and what is happening now.

The world system influences our parents to teach us to deal in reality. Reality highlights our limitations, while imagination overcomes limitations. We are also taught that it's not practical to address our dreams or even to dream. We are so busy being successful that we have forgotten that imagination is our birthright, a gift and blessing from God. Imagination must become a place where there are no boundaries or limitations. To be a successful steward you have to allow the power of imagination to work in your life. If not, your belief in reality, i.e. whatever your senses tell you, will not only limit you physically, but limit your access to this much-needed spiritual power. That's why prayer is important; it addresses your past, present, and future. Prayer changes the effects of your past, impacts the events of your present, and empowers and constructs your future.

After hearing the Word of the Lord, I immediately repented and sat down to imagine, and information began to flow to me unlike it had over the previous few months! Through imagination, I received creative material and strength to proceed to the next step, visualization.

Visualization If imagination is comparable to paint and canvas, then visualization is the act of painting what we want. I define visualization as the formation of specific images or concepts of what is not actually present to the senses. Imagination is the creative material, while visualization shapes the material according to your desire and goals. Jesus says in John 10:34, "Is it not written in your law, 'I said, "You are gods"'?" (NKJV). I believe that we are gods in the sense that we possess the capability to visualize and create like the True and Living God does, an example of which you are holding in your hand in the form of this book. The Stewardship Model was nothing more than a group of ideas until coupled with the power of imagination, the direction of visualization, and the focus of goals.

Goals Goal focus provides a constant reminder of where you want to go, giving your imagination a picture or destination to focus on. A goal contains a destination, but it is much more. A goal is your guide, your strength, and at times your encouragement. A misconception many people have about goals is that they should be written on paper and forgotten. This misconception contributes to the misunderstanding of how goals work. Goal focus keeps you going when you want to quit. Many people write down goals but don't review them as encouragement when the going gets tough. They tend to focus on the problems encountered en route to their goal. Always remember, goal focus keeps you going, but problem focus makes you want to quit.

The children of Israel while en route to their God-established goal encountered setbacks to completing their journey to the Promised Land. Instead of focusing on their goal and their God, they instead chose to focus on their problems. Exodus 3:8 and 16:2-3 states,

v8 So I have come down to deliver them out of the hand of the

Egyptians, and to bring them up from that land to a good and large land, to a land flowing with milk and honey, to the place of the Canaanites and the Hittites and the Amorites and the Perizzites and the Hivites and the Jebusites.
v2 Then the whole congregation of the children of Israel complained against Moses and Aaron in the wilderness.
v3 And the children of Israel said to them, "Oh, that we had died by the hand of the Lord in the land of Egypt, when we sat by the pots of meat and when we ate bread to the full! For you have brought us out into this wilderness to kill this whole assembly with hunger" (NKJV).

As a result of setbacks, the Children of Israel murmured and/or wanted to return to Egypt. That's what problem focus will do: it will prompt you to complain and wish you were back in easier times. That is how the devil operates. The devil wants you to take your eyes off of God and focus on setbacks. The devil hopes to create a belief that God is unfaithful, completing your goal is impossible, your talent is inadequate for the situation, and so much more. How many of you have wanted to do something, like re-enroll in school, but have found many excuses not to: I'm not smart enough, I work too many hours, I can't afford it, I have a family, etc. If this sounds like you, then you have stopped focusing on the goal but have begun to focus on the problems/limitations (reality). It has been my experience that the proper response to seemingly insurmountable setbacks is to remain focused on your goal, to imagine, and to seek God through prayer. Moses provides an example of the proper response to setbacks in Exodus 15:23-25:

v23 Now when they came to Marah, they could not drink the waters of Marah, for they were bitter. Therefore the name of it was called Marah.
v24 And the people complained against Moses, saying, "What shall we drink?"
v25 So he cried out to the Lord, and the Lord showed him a tree. When he cast it into the waters, the waters were made sweet (NKJV).

I can't count the number of times I felt like quitting this book project. It seemed that there were so many problems, but once I re-focused my attention toward my goal, imagined successful completion, and sought the Lord's guidance through prayer, what seemed impossible became possible. To accomplish your goals is not a matter of "how", but a matter of "why". Peter walked on water because of a why (He wanted to go to Jesus), not a how. He didn't know how (to walk on water), but his why was his reason.

I believe that God wants us to give Him a reason, and He will make a way. Listed below are descriptions of characteristics of goals. They are believable, conceivable, doable, well defined, tied to a timetable, desirable, measurable, and attainable.

Believable Belief is simply mentally accepting something as true. Belief is an essential part of acquiring or achieving any goal. Belief makes even prayer effective. (James 1:68)

Conceivable Your goal must be something that can be created with the correct materials.

Doable Your goal must be something that can be done by you.

Well-defined It must be clearly stated and/or within distinguishable limits. Writing down your goal helps you define it and know when you achieve it.

On a timetable This helps you prioritize your actions. Without a timetable, you may become distracted by other things and lose focus on, or even abandon, achieving your goals. Establishing and adhering to a timetable helps prevent you from getting distracted.

Desirable Goals have to be desirable. Without desire you can become easily tempted to quit when faced with difficulty. Desire keeps you going when circumstances say quit.

Measurable Goals must be measurable to determine when the goal has been met or is in the process of being met. For example, a goal of being rich is not measurable, but a goal of possessing assets valued in excess of one million dollars by the end of this year is measurable.

Attainable If you can't attain the goal, then why set it in the first place? Many people don't realize the importance and advantage of establishing a goal as a means to success. Without goals your destination becomes hit or miss. Accomplishing your objective is left up to chance or the priority it's given on someone else's timetable.

Emotions Many fortunes large and small have been affected by emotional responses. Why? People tend to make financial decisions based on their emotions, not their minds. For example, investors who invest quickly in something promising a greater than average return, because they didn't want to miss the upswing, whether or not they knew what they were doing, is an example of people who respond emotionally.

Matthew 25:24-25 presents another example of emotional thinking. The lazy steward says, "Lord, I knew thee that thou art an hard man, reaping where thou hast not sown, and gathering where thou hast not strawed: and I was afraid, and went and hid thy talent in the earth: lo, there thou hast that is thine" (KJV). The lazy steward's financial transactions were decided or influenced by his emotions or emotional past. The influence on present action by past emotions is the trademark of emotional thinking. It's obvious from the steward's choice of words that something similar had occurred in the past, and he was reliving those emotions in the present. Unfortunately, by reacting as he did, the steward approached his financial future by referencing a past emotion.

The passage doesn't indicate that only the lazy steward, all, or none of the stewards experienced a harsh past encounter with the master. The passage doesn't indicate they were treated any differently aside from the fact that they each received a different amount of talents.

Had the lazy steward taken time to think analytically about the master's objective, he would have done at least what the master suggested in verse 27. "Thou oughtest therefore to have put my money to the exchangers, and then at my coming I should have received mine own with usury" (KJV). By using his rational mind the servant would have acknowledged his fear and devised a means to overcome the fear and complete his task, a task, I might add, he was fully capable of completing. Instead, all that he was given was taken away from him and given to another, because he acted on an impulse.

Here are some questions you should ask for emotional self-assessment.

a) Do my feelings dictate how I handle money?
b) Do I fear prosperity?
c) Do I make emotional financial decisions?
d) Generally, are my financial transactions reactive?
e) Am I approaching my financial future through my emotional past?

If you answered "yes" to any of these questions, then it's quite possible that you have trained yourself to make your financial transactions based on the way you feel at the moment. The influence on present action by past emotion is emotional thinking. Persistent thinking on a matter influences our emotions. Emotions are our responses to our thoughts. Emotions are designed to assist our thoughts into becoming reality for us.

For example, if you think that you are overweight, after a while you become sad, or depressed, and depressed people tend to eat. Once you eat and receive comfort from eating, then you think that you are overweight, creating and fostering an un-ending cycle. Emotions are the seed for motivating you to move or holding you still. The importance of being aware of your emotions is to use the emotion to trace it back to the thought and correct it. You should take strategic measures to avoid impulsive reactions. Here are some suggestions to help you.

a) Stop, calm down, and think before you act.
b) Determine what the problem is.
c) Determine the cause of the problem.
d) Determine as many alternative solutions as possible.
e) Determine the best solution.
f) Implement the best solution.

Desires Have you ever desired something? It was more powerful than a simple want. It was something that you desperately had to have. Did you receive it? Most likely you did, because if you desired it hard enough you refused to quit until your desire was satisfied. Desire is the fruit of the seeds of emotion. To desire is to long for; to wish for earnestly; to covet. Desire motivates us to move or hold still. Desire pulls things to us and us to things.

Let's review the parable of the talents for an example of the power of desire. Each steward possessed the ability to increase the value of the talents entrusted to him. Each good steward's desire was to manage and increase what his master had given him, while the lazy steward's only desire was to give the master back his original investment. The lazy steward says that because the master's character scared him, he decided to bury the talent in a hole. This highlights two points about desire.

a) You can give only as much as you desire to give, and
b) The strongest motivation for success comes from within.

Regardless of our perception of God's character, our desire should be, since we received our master's good gifts for a lifetime, to act righteously and with maximum effort to return them better than they were given. We can only speculate whether or not the good stewards feared the master. We can, however, realistically conclude that their internal motivation to succeed was stronger than their fear.

Motivation is simply that which inspires you to move. Fear, in most cases, immobilizes you or at best causes you to hesitate. When we compare their responses, we see that the good stewards went and traded with their resources, while the lazy steward dug in the ground and hid his lord's money (Matthew 25:18 NKJV). This response highlights the effect of a poor belief system. The components of poor belief systems consist of negative thoughts, emotions, desires, and actions. It was the lazy steward's thoughts about the master that caused him to experience the emotion of fear. This emotional experience created a desire within him to return what the master had given him. This desire resulted in his action of hiding the talent in the ground.

Actions What is inside of you manifests through your actions. The good stewards possessed a servant's mentality, believing it was their responsibility to manage and increase the master's goods. The lazy steward possessed a slave's mentality. If not instructed, a slave will expend no effort and feel no responsibility to complete a task. All stewards have this in common: the Lord has graciously entrusted to each of us at least one talent. Matthew 25 shows us three responses to our receiving that talent from God: Active (steward gives maximum effort and output), Passive (steward gives minimum effort and output), and Non-Active (steward gives no effort and output). Matthew 25:29 says, "For to everyone who has, more will be given, and he will have abundance; but from him who does not have, even what he has will be taken away" (NKJV).

God expects us to increase and share His talent with others, and God will reward us for doing so. The Bible says that the good stewards immediately went and traded double the original talents (Matthew 25:16-17, KJV). This is an example of a viewpoint I call **Active Response**. Stewards possessing an active response viewpoint are described in verse 29: "For to everyone who has *[practices active response]*, more will be given, and he will have abundance . . ."(NKJV, explanations added). With active response a steward gives maximum effort and output. This is a righteous response, one that God rewards in all of his servants who possess it. Hear what God says to the good servants:

v21 His lord said to him, "Well done, good and faithful servant; you were faithful over a few things, I will make you ruler over many things. Enter into the joy of your lord" (NKJV).

Conversely, God will punish us for not increasing our talent and for holding it back from others. This is what I call **Non-Active Response**. With non-active response a steward gives no effort and output. Stewards possessing a non-active response viewpoint are described in verse 29: "but from him who does not have *[practices non-active response]*, even what he has will be taken away" (NKJV, emphasis added). Listen to how God feels about the steward who responded non-actively.

v26 "But his lord answered and said to him, 'You wicked and lazy servant, you knew that I reap where I have not sown, and gather where I have not scattered seed'" (NKJV).

Sounds harsh? I don't think so: not using your talent is the height of wickedness and laziness. What other words could be used to describe someone who refused to share God's gift to the world? The Bible teaches, "Every good gift and every perfect gift is from above, and comes down from the Father of lights, with whom there is no variation or shadow of turning" (James 1:17, NKJV). Therefore, to despise your gift and not share it with the world denies everyone the benefit from something good, and as you can see by God's response, He views it as wickedness.

Finally, there is what I call the **Passive Response**. The passive response is an acknowledgement of the importance of a response, but it produces only the minimum response. God himself describes this response in verse 27, "So you ought to have deposited my money with the bankers *[produced the minimum response]*, and at my coming I would have received back my own with interest" (NKJV, emphasis added). This type of response won't cause you to be punished. But it also doesn't reward you with rulership over much.

Each of us has a talent or ability that satisfies the needs of someone else. Your holding this book is proof of that. For every talent satisfying the needs of others, there are many buried in the ground. The cause? Fear. Fear that your talent isn't good enough or that the market would be unwilling to accept it. There are singers who sing uplifting songs, and writers who write encouraging words, who are afraid that the market has no use for their product/service. Belief that your talent/ability offers something valuable is what separates successful stewards from not so successful ones.

Describe Your Talent

We all have talents. What separates the person who successfully uses those talents, and the person who doesn't, is belief. Belief is the mental acceptance of something as true. By believing in your talent you mentally accept that:

a) Your talent is unique.
b) Your talent is valuable.

Your Talent is Unique In all walks of life there are successful people. There are some who are successful actors, singers, models, teachers, doctors, etc. What contributes to the success of these individuals? Their unique talents. Each successful person who has learned to believe in the uniqueness of his talent has discovered a key ingredient to success. People who believe in their unique talents don't limit them. Belief in talents will bring people to the forefront of life. The servant who was given two talents didn't complain that he didn't have five talents like the first servant. He believed in the uniqueness of his gift and as a result doubled his talents. Unlike the second servant, the third servant didn't believe in his unique talent, was paralyzed with fear, and subsequently lost it. How many of you are paralyzed with fear and discouragement, because you don't sing like Whitney, dunk like Jordan, write like Maya, or preach like Bishop Jakes? We as Americans have to be careful. Most of us have been taught that if you can't be number one, then being number two is not worth the effort. The secret to success is not necessarily who is number one, but going as far as your talent will take you. We need a paradigm shift to stop viewing uniqueness as a weakness and instead claim it as a strength.

Your Talent is Valuable Realization of and belief in the uniqueness of your talent brings awareness of your talent by others. The scriptures provide two contrasting examples of such awareness, in the lives of Joseph and Gideon. Joseph's story begins in Genesis 37. Joseph was the favorite son of his father, Jacob. As a result of this favor, Joseph's brothers grew jealous of him and sold him into slavery. Eventually, he ended up in the employ of an Egyptian officer named Potiphar. Genesis 39:3-5 describes what happened to Joseph when his master became aware of Joseph's talent.

v3 And his master saw that . . . the Lord made all he did to prosper in his hand.
v4 So Joseph found favor in his sight, and served him. Then he made him overseer of his house, and all that he had he put in his authority.
v5 So it was, from the time that he had made him overseer of his house and all that he had, that the Lord blessed the Egyptian's house for Joseph's sake; and the blessing of the Lord was on all that he had in the house and in the field" (NKJV).

Notice verse 3, where Joseph's master saw that the Lord was with him and that the Lord made all he did to prosper in his hand. Potiphar realized Joseph's uniqueness, and Joseph and his talent became very valuable. A similar situation arose when Pharaoh dreamed a dream (Gen. 41:15) and became aware of Joseph's unique talent to interpret dreams.

After interpreting the dream, Joseph became so valuable to Pharaoh that he was elevated to the number two position in the kingdom. The Bible tells what a man's gift will do for him, in Proverbs 18:16, "A man's gift makes room for him, and brings him before great men" (NKJV). While it's true that your gift will bring you before great men, only your belief in that gift will keep you in their presence. In the parable of the talents in Matthew 25:14, the man called his own servants to himself. Each servant's gift made room for him. The end of this passage paints a different picture entirely. Because the last servant didn't believe in the uniqueness of his talent, and didn't increase the gift, he was cast into the outer darkness [v.30], out of the presence of the great man. In light of this information, it would behoove each of us to believe in our talents so that when our gifts make room for us and bring us before great men, we will remain in their presence and not be cast out.

In contrast to Joseph, Gideon (Judges 6:12-13) didn't believe in his talent.

v12 And the Angel of the Lord appeared to him, and said to him, "The LORD is with you, you mighty man of valor!"
v13 Gideon said to Him, "O my lord, if the Lord is with us, why then has all this happened to us? And where are all His miracles which our fathers told us about, saying, 'Did not the Lord bring us up from Egypt?' But now the Lord has forsaken us and delivered us into the hands of the Midianites" (NKJV).

When the Angel of the Lord spoke to Gideon, he identified a spiritual talent, God's presence, since during that time the Bible doesn't indicate that God spoke to anyone else save Gideon, nor does it indicate that God was with anyone else save Gideon. Undaunted by Gideon's disbelief, the Angel of the Lord spoke again to Gideon:

v14 Then the Lord turned to him and said, "Go in this might of yours, and you shall save Israel from the hand of the Midianites. Have I not sent you?"
v15 So he said to Him, "O my Lord, how can I save Israel? Indeed my clan is the weakest in Manasseh, and I am the least in my father's house" (NKJV).

The Lord now tells Gideon that his talent is so valuable that he will save Israel from the hand of the Midianites. Again, Gideon's lack of belief surfaces, this time in the valuation of his talent. Despite the Lord's revelation of his value, Gideon says to the Lord that his clan is the weakest (least valuable) in Manasseh, and he is the least (valuable) in his father's house (Judges 6:15). How's that for not believing in your value? We respond today as Gideon did, when God tells us how great we are and that He is with us. We tell God that we are poor or come from a poor family, have never done anything great, can't do it like so and so, don't have enough money or talent or whatever excuse we feel is available to lean on to doubt what God says about us and what we can do. The world will respond based on the value you assign your talent. Can you imagine, if Gideon hadn't asked for a sign, Israel's deliverance from the Midianites could have been delayed, or worse, never have occurred? All because he didn't believe in his talent or the value of that talent. How many of you may be delaying the deliverance for your families, churches, etc., all because you don't believe the talent God says you have to offer is valuable?

Deliver Your Talent

I spent the early part of my practice lamenting the fact that I didn't have hordes of clients knocking down my door. Later, I realized that I hadn't moved past interest in operating a business to being committed to operating a business. Interested people don't put their whole heart, money, and time into their business, committed people do. People had a need for financial consulting, but printing thousands of business cards and leaving them in the box was not the answer. I needed to identify my services, develop them, and take what I had to offer to the marketplace.

Having the best product or greatest talent does nothing for you if it's not in the marketplace. The lazy steward discovered this first hand. Because he hid from the market, the results of hiding from the market were his - no increase. Only he and the master knew that he had the talent, because he buried it in the ground. The other stewards immediately went out with the talents they had to offer, and the market responded in kind. There is a principle involved here: To receive from the market, you must let the market know what you have to offer. Please be aware that I'm not suggesting that, if you have a talent, you jump into a business without developing the level of competence the marketplace demands from you. Each good steward possessed ability (competence) and took that to the marketplace, and it responded in kind.

Summary

Discern your assets: Mental, Physical, Social, and Spiritual Assets

Discover your talent: Inquire of God, Learn through suffering,
Ask yourself questions

Develop your talent: Thoughts, Emotions, Desires, and Actions

Describe your talent: Unique, Valuable

Deliver your talent

Chapter 4
Financial Management: Money Viewpoints

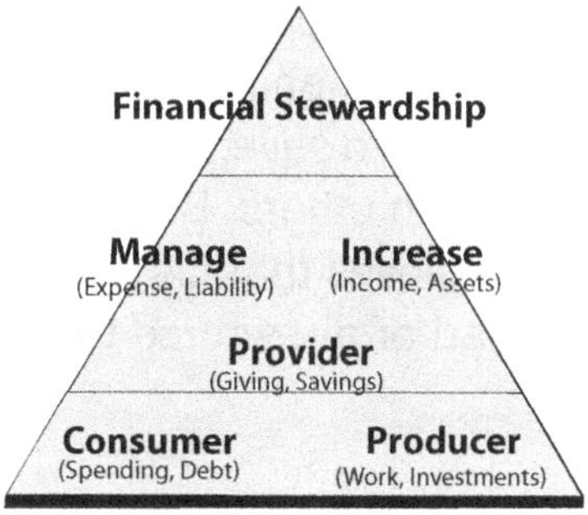

A **Consumer** is defined as one who consumes (economic) goods.
A **Provider** is defined as one who supplies (economic) goods for sustenance or support.
A **Producer** is defined as one who produces (economic) goods.

Each of us views our finances through one or more of these viewpoints. By viewpoint, I mean the way a person expects to use any available money. For example, say you found $100, what would you do? If you have a consumer viewpoint, your first thought would be to buy something or pay a bill. A provider would perhaps save it or even give a portion of it to someone else in need. A producer would use that money to somehow accumulate even more money. To truly prosper, you must learn that there is a season for everything: a season to consume, a season to provide, and a season to produce. The action in which you operate most often gives insight into your main financial viewpoint. Your main financial viewpoint is your primary perception of money. The way you developed this perception is directly related to your most memorable money incident (if you were not taught) or the viewpoint that was taught and reinforced by your parents' financial actions or inactions.

An adherence to, or under-valuation of, the other financial viewpoints directly affects the way you operate in your main viewpoint. For example, my main viewpoint is that of a provider, and to be the most efficient and effective provider, I need to value the benefits of the consumer and producer viewpoints. I have to manage spending and debt paying as well as maximize the creation of income through work and investing. A provider who doesn't value the other viewpoints is apt to become a miser or irresponsible giver. Why? Because when our focus is limited to our main viewpoint, it is reinforced to such a degree that the strength of our main viewpoint becomes our financial weakness. A miser is simply a saver who has gone to extremes to save. He saves no matter the cost to his relationship with God or with others. Because he has no concept of the producer viewpoint, he believes that his money is a scarce resource and must be hoarded, instead of a resource that is the seed for investments.

The items listed in each category for use of money represent a sample of the items contained in each viewpoint.

Consumer Viewpoint

The Consumer Viewpoint consists of spending and debt payments. Spending includes money you spend on yourself or others that you are not obligated by agreement to spend. For example, this would include money spent on entertainment, jewelry, and clothes. Debt paying represents money you spend on obligations. Valuing the other money viewpoints helps the consumer control his money. Unless a person establishes this value, money becomes fuel for his desires or his debts, fuel that is neither conserved (saved) nor renewed (increased).

Spender Spenders with a myopic viewpoint of money want to acquire whatever the world has to offer them. How they acquire it is a secondary concern. If cash is unavailable, but their credit qualifies for what they want, then they are going to buy it: anything from clothes to cars to vacations, and the list goes on and on. Consumers believe that saving for themselves or giving to others is impossible. They believe that they have money available to be spent on consumer items or for paying bills, an outlook that closes the door to the blessing most of them so desperately need.

In Mark 12:41-44 Jesus was watching the rich people put money in the treasury (offering). He observed a poor widow woman giving two mites into the offering. Now, a mite was the Jews' smallest coin, equivalent to less than our penny. Why would Jesus notice and make mention of such a small gift? I mean, during this time in history no one was as little admired as a poor, widowed woman. I believe Jesus drew attention to this gift to highlight the fact that even the smallest gift given by the lowest person in humanity's eyesight is valued and noticed by God. Giving, no matter the amount, still opens the door to increase, whether you have given of your abundance (what money was left over) or of your poverty (from money that you needed). Valuing the other viewpoints helps the consumer control his money. Without this valuation the consumer lets money become fuel for his desires, fuel that is neither conserved (saved) nor renewed (increased).

Debtor A debtor's money is spent on obligations. Debtors see only paying debt. The debt stands in front of opportunities to save, give, and invest. Debtors have become so consumed by debt that they make additional payments to reduce debt without investing some of their money for increase, giving, savings, or achieving personal goals. Putting money in one of these areas helps to remove the blinders that existing obligations place over your eyes. Obligations range from your monthly utility bill to your mortgage payment. Obligations are created by:

1) Overspending
2) Under-earning
3) Lack of planning

Overspending As mentioned earlier, spenders want to acquire what the world has to offer them. How they acquire it is a secondary concern. As a result of this thinking, spenders eventually spend beyond their resources, creating debt. This type of thinking affects rich and poor alike. Note the parable of the Prodigal Son, found in Luke 15:

v11 Then He said: "A certain man had two sons.
v12 "And the younger of them said to his father, 'Father, give me the portion of goods that falls to me.' So he divided to them his livelihood.
v13 "And not many days after, the younger son gathered all together, journeyed to a far country, and there wasted his possessions with prodigal living.
v14 "But when he had spent all, there arose a severe famine in that land, and he began to be in want" Luke 15:11-14(NKJV).

Overspending without regard to managing and creating money leads to debt and want. In modern times, the spender's vision is so distorted that despite his current overspending and/or increasing debt, he feels that he deserves to spend something on himself for working so hard paying bills, thereby creating the cycle all over again.

Under-earning Under-earners aren't usually "big spenders," they simply lack the money necessary to meet their needs. This state of being arises from under-utilizing your talents whether through lack of belief or not realizing the true value that your talent brings, you allow yourself not to be properly compensated for what you do. When an individual or family doesn't earn enough money for their needs, those without an understanding of how financial matters operate can fall prey to lenders who offer money or extend credit to meet the shortfall.

Lack of Planning Incredible as it may sound, there are people who are marginal spenders at best, who earn enough money for their needs, but who have found themselves in debt. Why? Lack of planning. Many of you are, or know, someone who has encountered one unexpected event after another: the car needed extensive repairs, a medical condition required a temporary work stoppage, etc. Of course, while all of this is happening, the obligations mount. Without prior planning for these "unforeseen events of life" through insurance and/or savings, maintaining your current standard of living can easily cause you to go into debt.

Many people possess what I call “tunnel vision”. By tunnel vision, I mean that when looking at their future they view it through a tunnel, a tunnel that is straight and doesn’t have any twists or turns. A better example is a client I had who expected his financial outlook to remain the same. There was no plan for loss of job, loss of spouse, or any “event of life”. The parable of the ten virgins (Matthew 25:1-13) details the consequences of not preparing to the greatest extent possible for an “event of life”. In this parable a total of ten virgins were awaiting the arrival of the bridegroom. Five wise virgins planned for the arrival of the bridegroom by day or night, while the other five, the “foolish” virgins, were prepared only for the bridegroom’s arrival by day. But while his arrival was delayed, they went to sleep. Suddenly, at midnight the cry went out that the bridegroom was coming, and all the virgins prepared to go out to meet him, guided by their lamps. The five foolish virgins realized that they didn’t plan for his coming at night and suffered the dire consequence of being left behind.

I can’t stress enough the importance of financial planning. During my life I have been “grieved” hearing a few “testimonies” of people who gleefully travel the financial road of life without a plan, “depending on God”. Before you stop reading, let me explain. I sincerely believe with all of my heart that God is the God of miracles, provision, etc. There is no limit to what He can and will do for His children during a time of need or abundance. But I also believe that those who serve God and bless others carry a responsibility for navigating life, never independent of God, but using God’s previous provision without requiring immediate intervention by God (practicing only crisis/miracle dependence on God). By crisis/miracle dependence I mean standing still and watching the salvation of the Lord (Exodus 14:13) when we are capable of moving forward with Him. God didn’t write this book, I did, but I couldn’t have written it independently of him. I didn’t sit and wait for God to write it for me and then place my name on the cover. I had to proceed with my plan, and like Moses (Exodus 14:15-16), use what I had to go forward. During the famine (Genesis 41:53-54) Joseph had a plan; his family in Israel didn’t. Yet if Joseph hadn’t made plans and moved with God, both he and his family would have starved.

Lack of planning is sure to result in financial chaos. Make plans, increase your money, and manage your money to the Glory of God. Details on creating a financial plan are found in Chapter Four. Now let's continue to the next viewpoint in-depth, the Provider Viewpoint.

Provider Viewpoint

A provider seeks to provide for himself (saving) and/or others (giving) with what he has available. Saving is money for self or projects. Although considered an expense, savings, unlike other expenses, doesn't take away from you, it adds to you. Because saving adds to you, it is an essential part of any spending plan. Businesses have an account called Cost of Goods Sold, which tracks how much it costs them to produce the product that generates income for their company. The provider side of the management quadrant serves that role. The provider side records the amount of money available to increase you. By managing your money to allot for saving and giving, you gradually expand your consumer viewpoint to include the provider viewpoint. Some people may say that because a provider provides for himself he should be described as a consumer. The main difference between a consumer and a provider is the fact that a consumer seeks to acquire what the world has to offer, while a provider seeks to benefit the world (his surroundings) with the money he has presently to offer.

Producer Viewpoint

A producer seeks to benefit the world (his surroundings) by what he does. He is extremely focused on increasing. A producer will work long hours without complaint to increase financially. The more he works, it seems the more he wants to work. Producers who invest share similar traits. They use any available economic resource to increase. Commonly, producers produce at the expense of managing their money. Because of this extreme focus on increasing, producers can suffer from lack of financial management. I've served as a consultant for producers who pay their bills late, incur late charges, and are generally lax in management of their money. One in particular had such an emphasis on making money that he found himself unable to manage the money he already had. His inability to manage money was the culprit behind his never being able to properly benefit from his labors. This contributed to the "burnout" feeling that he would always complain of; that led to feeling that he could never acquire enough money to rest. Another way of stating that is, producers are so focused on producing that they aren't aware of what happened to the money they have already produced. Possessing this viewpoint contributes to "burnout" and is a factor, I believe, in producing shorter life spans in men.

There are other producers who have increased so much that they don't know what to do with their money. The Bible chronicles this type of producer in the parable of the rich fool located in Luke 12:

v16 "The ground of a certain rich man yielded plentifully.
v17 "And he thought within himself, saying, 'What shall I do, since I have no room to store my crops?'
v18 "So he said, 'I will do this: I will pull down my barns and build greater, and there I will store all my crops and my goods.
v19 "'And I will say to my soul, "Soul, you have many goods laid up for many years; take your ease; eat, drink, and be merry"'" Luke 12:16-19 (NKJV).
This rich man bypassed his responsibility to be a true provider, and instead he embraced selfishness.

A modern rich man, Bill Gates, in my opinion, is a producer who chose an alternate decision. In the past, people have criticized that despite his great wealth, Mr. Gates has not been very charitable. Personally, I don't believe that Mr. Gates is greedy. As a producer he believes that he can most benefit the world by what he does, which is help computer users all over the world get the most out of their computers. His becoming the richest man in the world is a byproduct of this belief. As a result of widening his viewpoint, Mr. Gates, along with his wife, have since contributed hundreds of millions of dollars through their foundation, to benefit the world.

Conflict of Viewpoints

Most of us view money differently from some of our friends, and at no other time is this more evident than when people get married. Except in rare instances, you and your spouse will initially view finances differently. This explains why the most relationship-threatening problems couples have are in dealing with money. Prior to the marriage each partner usually handled money according to only one, possibly two, of the aforementioned financial viewpoints. So when they marry and are confronted with foreign financial viewpoints, conflict erupts. What marriage wouldn't experience conflict when one spouse's financial viewpoint is to work, work, and work some more for money, while the other spouse's viewpoint of money is to spend, or in more simplified terms, "have money, will spend it". One spouse is constantly shoveling in, while the other is constantly shoveling out. Eventually something will break, and usually it's one spouse's patience. Another example may be the spouse who, if necessary, will literally "give the shirt off of his back". Now a person who firmly believes that money should be spent on family needs first would have a problem if the other spouse is constantly giving of his resources to others, before meeting his needs and/or the needs of his family. Before you "providers" get angry with me, let me repeat, there is nothing inherently wrong with any of the three viewpoints. Problems arise when you embrace a myopic focus on your primary money viewpoint, all the time, regardless of the situation. For example, those who have an extreme viewpoint of production have a tendency to become/appear workaholic/greedy. Those who focus only on consumption have a tendency to become poor/indebted. Those who focus only on providing have a tendency to become miserly/irresponsible.

Balanced Viewpoint

What was your first memory of money as a child? Were you taught that money was something to be spent as soon as you received it, or did you perhaps learn that you were supposed to work and/or use your wits to accumulate money for yourself? I'm sure there are still others who learned to give until it hurts (literally!). Remember, the Bible tells us in

Proverbs 22:6-7 to "Train up a child in the way he should go, And when he is old he will not depart from it. The rich rules over the poor, And the borrower is servant to the lender" (NKJV). Which were you taught to be, the lender or the borrower? Each one of us acquired one or more of these viewpoints as children. This training from our parents or other financial role models helps us to embark on the path to riches or the path to poverty. There are people I know who write post-dated checks until money arrives, and they are inadvertently teaching their children to do the same. This vicious cycle can be stopped with you and your children. When they receive money, ask them what they will do with it, and the answer will give you an indication of how they were taught by you or someone else.

The goal of the Stewardship Model is to blend all viewpoints to eliminate the potential danger of operating solely in individual viewpoints. A balanced money viewpoint enhances the effectiveness of your primary viewpoint. For example, a consumer who understands the importance of expanding his awareness to include providing and increasing will have more money available to spend, be a more effective consumer, and be less likely to get in debt. This emancipates you from the spending/debt-paying cycle, because you are regaining control of your money.

As I mentioned earlier, producers are extremely focused on increasing, focused to the extent that many aren't aware of what happened to the money they have already produced. Producers who possess a balanced viewpoint have acquired a purpose for their efforts: savings for themselves, giving to others, and permitting themselves to spend some of the money they have produced. Where there was once unending financial increase that eventually would have led to burnout, there is now a purpose that renews them and prevents burnout. As wood is to fire, so purpose is to the producer. We must learn that there is a time to produce, a time to consume, and a time to provide. The way we handle our finances should be a reflection of all three viewpoints. A balanced money philosophy is the foundation upon which Financial Stewardship operates.

Financial Management and Your Viewpoint

Identifying your viewpoint is the initial step in proper money management. It helps you discover the cause of potential problems that extend beyond simply having more expenses than income. Your spending plan will show only how you use your money, not the reason you handle money the way you do. Following either a spending plan, a budget, or no budget are ways you manage money, and your money viewpoint is the reason you handle your money the way you do. It's been said often that we tend to see the world in shades of black, white, or gray, and we act accordingly.

The same case can be made for the financial viewpoints. Viewing money a certain way influences how you manage your money. Managing money with either a generalized spending plan, a budget, or no budget places the onus on the individual possessing discipline to spend less than is earned. For those lacking discipline, this doesn't work because their individual viewpoints are not addressed in the plan or budget. Therefore, personalizing your budget becomes easier because it is created with your financial viewpoint in mind.

For example, a person has difficulty adhering to her budget. Her income is sufficient to meet her needs, but she finds herself shopping excessively. She's not compelled to shop, she possesses a consumer viewpoint. Because she possesses this viewpoint, and it was not addressed in her budget, she feels depressed due to her lack of discipline. In fact, by allocating a portion of the money available for the purpose of consumption to the things she likes, she can get her budget better aligned with the way she views money.

Getting Started

As with any journey, one must assess where he is before determining where he is going and the means by which he will get there. Using the management quadrant, determine where you are by first analyzing the amount/percentage of finances on the consumer side in relation to the provider side. This is called Average Propensity. The goal of figuring Average Propensity is to calculate the percentage of your total dollars used for spending, giving, debt paying, and savings. The destination (minimum standard) one should strive for is 80% consumer side and 20% provider side. The following chart provides an example of the ratio.

Consumer	Provider
5-15% Spending	10-15% Giving
55-75% Debt paying	10-15% Saving

Review your finances and record the amount spent for each category. Then, divide each amount by the sum of your finances to arrive at your ratio. For example, let's say your monthly income is $10.00. The following is the way you reported your breakdown: Spending $2, Debt paying $7, Saving $.50 and Giving $.50. Your money management chart would look like this:

Consumer	Provider
2/10 or 20% Spending	.50/10 or 5% Giving
7/10 or 70% Debt paying	.50/10 or 5% Saving

Based on the results of the ratio, this individual spends a whopping combination of 20% of his inflow on himself and 70% of his inflow on debt paying. Although debt paying in this case also includes normal household expenses, I believe that the excessively high spending ratio contributes to the high-debt paying ratio. This person does give, but not enough to become a true provider. A true biblical provider should have a minimum ratio of 10%.

I would suggest that this individual either reduce spending, reduce debt paying, or reduce a combination of both categories to an amount equaling 10% of inflow, with that difference shifted to the provider side.

The following is another example of the stewardship ratio. Let's say there is another person with the following breakdown: Spending $6, debt paying $3, Giving $1, and savings $0. This equals a total inflow of $10.00. The money management chart would look like this:

Consumer	Provider
6/10 or 60% Spending	1/10 or 10% Giving
3/10 or 30% Debt paying	0 or 0% Saving

There are many people in the Body of Christ whose finances are reflected in the above ratios (or worse). These individuals don't have because they spend too much money on themselves and/or on others in proportion to their total inflow. They may (as in this case) give, but any increase is offset by an increase in the amount of money used for spending.

<u>Special Note</u>: Many of you may not know if you have increased because your spending/debt paying grows in proportion with any increase in cash flow. Without financial tracking, any increase you receive is not perceived as one.

The previous diagrams are not at all the only patterns of the financial status. There are some whose ratios may be even better. At this time, my management chart looks like this.

Consumer	Provider
.50/10 or 5%	1.5/10 or 15%
Spending	Giving
6.5/10 or 65%	1.5 or 15%
Debt paying	Saving

I have learned that the less money spent on consumption and debt payment without sacrificing personal needs for shelter, food, clothing, and other basic necessities of life, the more is available to be "deposited" on giving and saving toward investment. Therefore, I'm constantly striving to spend the money on the consumption/debt paying side efficiently, that I may increase money "deposited" on the giving/saving side. It's a natural (God-intended) progression to provision that provides an opportunity to fulfill the other crucial portion of stewardship. That portion, which will be discussed later, is Increase.

In the succeeding chapters I will discuss the two categories of the consumer viewpoint: **spending** and **debt paying**.

Summary

Consumer Viewpoint

Spend
Pay Debts

Causes of Debt

Spend too much
Earn too little
Fail to plan

Provider Viewpoint

Save
Give

Producer Viewpoint

Work
Invest

Balanced Viewpoint

Give 10%
Save 10%
Consume 80%

Chapter 5 Consumer Viewpoint: Spending

Shop 'til You Drop

What is spending? It's defined as paying out or using up money. To be more specific, spending was when you stopped by the bookstore and bought this book!! Everybody spends in some way or another; however, not everyone spends the same way and for the same reasons. These spending differences can either be the stepping-stones to prosperity or cause one to teeter on the brink of financial collapse. For some of you, spending is a way to alleviate sorrow, i.e., a pick-me-up. For others it's a means of independence or power. You may shop based on your feelings or on the amount of money you have. Some of you may even shop based on the money you don't have (credit).

Spending is relative to the individual; therefore, the amount you spend should be also. I've found that percentage-spending limits can be too restrictive for some people. Could you imagine Bill Gates' Financial Advisor counseling him not to spend more than 10% of his income on himself? There must be a blanket thought which can be tailored to individuals, and there is. I would suggest the following rule: You are spending too much when the items and lifestyle you buy (desire) become more pleasurable and important to you than the journey you are undertaking (financial stability/independence). Where do you want to go? What do you want to accomplish? What are some of the things you need money to accomplish? Your financial plan is your guide. It helps you allocate money to achieve the goals and values that are important to you. Remember, to get where you need to be financially, you must learn to enjoy the journey.

If you would recall the story of the children of Israel, they desired fleshpots (Exodus 16:3) and found more pleasure/importance in fleshpots than in the journey to a land flowing with milk and honey. The nature of the journey provides ample opportunity for pleasures. When God took the Israelites on the journey, He knew there would be things and conditions they wanted and it would be by traveling the particular route they were on that their desire for pleasures could be met, as in Exodus 15:27.

If you are journeying to financial independence/stability, then that journey will provide opportunity for spending. As you begin to organize your finances and manage properly, money will arise for spending. When you consistently buy things more pleasurable than the journey, then you are on the road to creating debt. The journey then becomes marred with problems. The goal should be not to stop spending, but to change bad habits associated with spending. With every cause there is an effect. If our spending is based on bad habits (impulse buying, etc.), then we will realize the effect of such actions (disorganized finances, debt, etc.).

Spending is not a problem and doesn't become a problem until spending is out of control. Remember, the real objective of having money is control. Any control lost in one financial category has a ripple effect in the others. If you decide to spend more than you earn, then your other three financial categories (savings, giving, and debt paying) will suffer. Your savings and giving will possibly decrease; your debt load will definitely increase. Excess spending indicates there is a lack either in you or in your money management.

Recognize Seeds for Overspending

As indicated in the previous section, with every cause there is an effect. When a farmer plants seed he expects those seeds to grow and produce. Likewise, if you allow the following seeds to take root in your financial plan, they will grow and produce a harvest of overspending and excessive indulgence.

1) Advertising
2) Expectations of Others
3) Love of Pleasure
4) Depression
5) Lack of Sound Financial Management

Advertising Advertising is the mother of overspending. One party (the advertiser) attempts to convince another party (the consumer) that the advertiser has the product that will meet a need and that the consumer has a need for the product the advertiser is selling. This is a means for television providing answers to your real or imagined problems, not promoting the searching out of answers on your part. In chapter three, I discussed a television-induced "hypnotic effect" called the alpha mode. While you are in this state, your mind's capacity to think is greatly reduced, and your susceptibility to suggestions or programming is greatly enhanced. Exposure to alpha waves allows electronic images to be beamed directly into your brain. Once planted, those images are extremely difficult to remove, which explains why as time passes you may have difficulty remembering your spouse's or parents' birthdays, but remember the jingle from a twenty-year-old commercial as if it were yesterday.

Advertising's ability to plant suggestions in your mind without your knowledge and awareness is a leading factor in the purchase of consumer products that you were enticed and deceived into believing you needed. You didn't know that you "needed" a Hummer until convincing television advertising told you that you did. Remember, advertisers wouldn't spend millions of dollars on advertising and endorsers if the return on their investment was not greater than the cost.

By itself, suggestive mental programming can be damaging to your personal finances, but coupled with lifestyle marketing, it leads to overspending that can quickly become a way of life. Lifestyle marketing is simply marketing a product that appeals to a person's activities, interests, and opinions. Once an advertiser has connected a product to you in this manner, you are sold. For example, if your opinion is that popular people wear Nike shoes priced at more than $100.00 a pair, and you want to be popular, then you will go to great lengths to get those shoes, no matter the cost to your personal finances. Credit card commercials are notorious for projecting a lifestyle that most people can't afford and can achieve only through the frequent use of consumer credit. Embracing this consumption lifestyle makes us increasingly vulnerable to the expectations of others and the love of pleasure.

Expectations of Others The expectations of others can lead people to suffer anxiety, worry, and overspending, especially during the holiday season. Many parents suffer from the gift expectations of their children, causing them to overspend. Unbeknownst to the parents, seeking to meet their children's desires which have been influenced by outside sources (advertising) can lead to money (financial) goals being ignored. Literally millions of people sink deeper into debt each passing year as a result of others' expectations. Even commercials are tailored with that thought in mind. For example, Valentine's Day is a boon for jewelry merchants. They project the illusion that you are not a good partner if you don't buy your significant other a gift–preferably diamonds. I experienced this personally with my wife. During our engagement period, I was in the process of purchasing my first home, and every penny was precious, but I was feeling extreme pressure from others (not her) to purchase an expensive diamond engagement ring. Finally, when I could take no more, I spoke with my then fiancée and stressed to her my point of view: purchasing a home now would set us on the path to generating wealth that I could use to purchase an engagement ring later. Fortunately, she understood, and I was able to proceed with the home purchase.

Love of Pleasure This is a craving for what in each situation can bring you fun and satisfaction. We are constantly bombarded by media that heighten the desire for, and expectation of, pleasure. As you indulge in these media - excessive television, games, movies, etc., it is likely that you'll become increasingly undisciplined and lazy. As discipline decreases, the ability to control finances and to generate finances decreases. People who love pleasure can become poor because they value pleasure more than prosperity. Because they value pleasure more than prosperity, they can pay more annually for premium cable channels and movies than they deposit in savings. No spending discipline yields no spending limits. No spending limits yield no money, because there is always something available to entice you. As the scripture indicates, "He that loveth pleasure shall be a poor man" (Proverbs 21:17, KJV).

A tangible expression of the Love of Pleasure is the Love of Possessions. This is the love of material things - cars, homes, jewelry, etc. Together with the love of pleasure, the love of possessions rarely offers long lasting satisfaction or fulfillment. The desire for more pleasure and new possessions, with no regard for cost, can cause you to exceed your financial level. We have become a short-cut society wanting dividends without the investment. Dividends come from investing, not from lack of investing. For example, by having your personal finances in order (investing), you should be able to afford the material possessions you desire, if that's your choice (dividend).

Depression This psychological state is a known instigator of overspending. There are some of you who may, when your spirits are low or you are feeling gloomy, view spending money as a therapeutic distraction. In most cases outside forces cause depression; money does not. So money should not be used to treat this condition. There may be instances when lack of money draws people into depression. Then it is highly probable that the culprit is actually not money but the lack of sound financial management.

Lack of Sound Financial Management This deficiency affects people who focus primarily on generating money and not on developing the ability to make money work for them (management). Remember, money is a faithful and obedient servant, but a poor master. If you don't manage your money, it will manage you. If your money is not your servant, then it will be the servant of someone else - creditors, other people, etc. God will not "free" you by giving you money, because your inability to manage money will continue to enslave you and keep you bound. Your inability to manage money will continue to enslave you and keep you bound until you learn strategies and methods that will cause you to increase and maintain your finances. Note the parable of the Prodigal Son, found in Luke 15:11-14:

v11 Then He said: "A certain man had two sons.
v12 "And the younger of them said to his father, 'Father, give me the portion of goods that falls to me.' So he divided to them his livelihood.
v13 "And not many days after, the younger son gathered all together, journeyed to a far country, and there wasted his possessions with prodigal living.
v14 "But when he had spent all, there arose a severe famine in that land, and he began to be in want.. . ." (NKJV).

Overspending without regard to managing and creating money leads to debt and want.

Identify Hindrances to Spending Correctly

For people to prosper and money to grow, money must be used from a position of control. That is, you control it by having it work for you. Money is not likely to flourish when it is possessed by a person who is hampered by the following hinderances.

a) Worry
b) Lack of financial control
c) Love of pleasure

Worry Worry over-emphasizes circumstances or the potential effect of circumstances in your life. If you pay attention only to the circumstances of your life, you yield control of your time, talent, and money. As you yield control there is no sense of direction, because you are pulled from circumstance to circumstance. All of your energies are then devoted to addressing the circumstance and not achieving the goal. For example, imagine a circumstance where you don't have enough money to pay your mortgage and you recently received a foreclosure notice. If you worry about the fact you may lose your home, this short-circuits the power inside of you (ability to generate money) and gives that power over to circumstances. Money can't flourish because you are thinking about what you don't want to happen (foreclosure), restricting money's flow. Several years ago I lost my job, and I worried over how my automobile loan and other things would be paid. Money was tight because I yielded control of my time, talent, and money over to the circumstance, resulting in my car being repossessed. Instead of focusing on developing the abilities which later allowed me to write this book, conduct seminars, and consult, among other things which could generate money, I ran around looking for jobs that were not suitable for my abilities, trying to maintain something that began to control me.

Lack of Financial Control Money is an excellent servant but a poor master. If you are not controlling your money, then it won't grow, because your money becomes a tool for someone else's use. One sure way to see if you lack financial control is to assess who prospers most from the money you earn. Are the retailers experiencing record sales from your lack of control, or are you experiencing the results of prosperity from your control (savings, investments, etc.). One surefire way to regain control of your money is to reduce the amount of television you watch. A high percentage of television programs are designed by networks and advertisers to stimulate your desire to consume products. With television being our main link to others in the world, we erroneously think that everything we view on television is reality. Studies have shown that the average American youth annually watches 1500 hours of commercials and television programming containing product placement. In comparison, the average American youth annually spends only 900 hours in school. It's no small wonder that excessive television is contributing to our transformation as a nation to consumers.

Love of Pleasure The Bible states in Proverbs 21:17 that he who loves pleasure will become poor. The main goal of this individual or "pleasure seeker" is to escape reality. An escape from reality is a means for avoiding the responsibilities of life, which include the sound management and increase of money. A lover of pleasure will not exercise sound judgment when it comes to financial matters. The love of pleasure forces you to seek after it at any cost. Pleasure seekers relinquish control of their money for the "high" of pleasure. It breaks my heart when I see people who, after exhausting their resources, turn to debt to continue the "high" of pleasure, unaware how this addiction spirals them into unbearable debt and poverty.

Spend Correctly

1. Spend based on what you value and what is really best for you. The basis of control in each spending category is your personal values and goals. Spending your money based on what everyone else is doing, wearing, and possessing can distract you from reaching your own goal. According to the A.C. Nielsen Co., the number of TV commercials seen by the average person by age 65 is 2 million. Developing your own values and goals will require you to separate yourself from media that impose themselves on you.

2. Continue spending, change habits. Spending doesn't become a problem until it is out of control. Impulse spending adds up to lost dollars when you become distracted from values and goals. Change your spending habits by striving to permanently eliminate impulse buying. In correcting spur-of-the-moment spending, try to use coupon shopping. Plan shopping in advance and make a list of the things you need to buy. Set a spending limit in accordance with your financial plan and spend with your plan in mind. When possible, research and compare prices on big-ticket items and negotiate for the best price.

3. Spend with your financial plan in mind. Remember, wanting things is not wrong. There are two ways of getting what you want: correctly and incorrectly. For example, if you want a $1000 mink coat, using your credit card when you are already in debt is the wrong way to get what you want. Saving for the coat, seeing it as a goal, is the right way. Purchasing something the wrong way tears you down (bad habits, debt, etc.) and doing it the right way builds you up (setting goals and achieving them). The fact that you can get what you want doesn't necessarily mean you are going about it the correct way. We were not placed on this planet to

use all of our financial resources to pay bills.

Create and Maintain a Workable Financial Plan

Contrary to most budgets, which place emphasis on expenses, the Map to Prosperity Plan puts primary focus on paying those you love first and providing for your goals. Paying those you love includes paying God through tithing, paying yourself through savings, and paying others through church offerings or charitable contributions. Paying those you love first is based on the principle found in Matthew 22:37-39:

v37 Jesus said to him, "'You shall love the LORD your God with all your heart, with all your soul, and with all your mind.'
v38 "This is the first and great commandment.
v39 "And the second is like it: 'You shall love your neighbor as yourself'" (NKJV).

Paying those you love first and providing for your goals gives you a sense of accomplishment and fulfillment that spending all of your money on bills never could.

Pay Those You Love First

1 Tithe	350.00
2 Savings	125.00
3 Offering	125.00

Goal focus provides a constant reminder of where you want to go, giving your imagination a picture or destination to focus on. A goal contains a destination, but it is much more. A goal is your guide, your strength, and at times your encouragement. A goal is believable, conceivable, doable, well defined, tied to a timetable, desirable, measurable, and attainable.

Goals

Goals-Intermediate	
5 New House Savings	50.00
6 Vacation	25.00
7 Mutual Fund	25.00

Necessity expenses are those items necessary for survival, such as food, clothing, electricity, water, and medical services.

Necessity	Expenses
8 Apartment	400.00
9 Car Insurance	50.00
10 Car	300.00
11 Food	200.00
12 Electricity	75.00
13 Water	50.00
14 Gas	100.00
15 Car Maintenance	30.00
16 Laundry/Cleaners	100.00
17 Phone	50.00
18 Clothes	50.00

Debt reduction consists of payments made to revolving credit obligations like credit card payments, and principal payments made to necessity expenses like your mortgage or automobile loan.

Desire expenses consist of those expenses that are not needs, but wants and luxuries. Wants are those items beyond the necessary that are desired for improved comfort and satisfaction. These vary according to individual interests, tastes, and lifestyles. Some examples include brand name clothing, brand name shoes, eating out, etc.

Luxuries are those items beyond wants. They indulge fantasies and dreams beyond those experienced by many. An example of a luxury for middle class people would be ownership of a private jet or several foreign cars. Of course, luxuries also vary according to individual interests and tastes.

Miscellaneous expenses consist of personal spending money for things like snacks and personal items for you or your spouse.

Debt Reduction/Desire Expenses/Miscellaneous	
20 Credit Card Payment	50.00
21 Husband Personal	50.00
22 Wife Personal	50.00
Total Expenses	2,255.00
Income/Salary	
Combined Annual Salary	35,000.00
Average Monthly Income	
(26 paydays)	2,485.56
Net Income	2,485.56
Net Expenses	(2,255.00)
Total Surplus	230.56

There are six steps to help you create and maintain a workable financial plan. They are:

1) Analyze your income and pay those you love first.
2) Write down your goals.
3) Analyze expenses.
4) Balance your income with your expenses.
5) Develop a spending plan (budget).
6) Adjust your plan to changes.

There are several steps to creating a workable plan. A financial plan must be quickly developed, based on biblical principles, and able to guide you to prosperity. Think of it as your map to achieving your goals. A real plan is not for limiting your spending so you can pay more to creditors. It's designed for you, by you. Money can be an emotional issue, so your plan should take your emotions into account.

Analyze your Income and Pay Those You Love First Write down all sources of income. If you are paid bi-weekly, I suggest that you record the income on your budget on a monthly basis. If your income varies, allocate more money to your monthly income budget in those months when there is surplus income.

Write Down Your Goals

Identify your goals A goal contains a destination that must be reached. A goal is something that is believable, conceivable, doable, desirable, just out of your reach, and measurable. Goals are written on paper and in your mind's eye. Goals contain timetables. It's timetables that separate goals from dreams.

Long-term goals can be accomplished in five or more years.
Intermediate goals can be accomplished in one to five years.
Short-term goals can be accomplished in less than one year.

Clarify your goals In determining your goal you must be specific. Don't be afraid. The only people who will see your financial plan are you and God. He's not going to tell anybody! He wants to help you achieve those God-given goals. God will never tell you to do something He's not willing to help you achieve, if you need help.

Categorize and rate your goals in order of importance It is more satisfying for you when you achieve first the goals that mean the most.

Act Now The longer you delay, the greater the likelihood of your not adhering to your financial plan.

Analyze Your Expenses

Write down all of your expenses. Include both fixed expenses (amounts that remain the same) and variable expenses (amounts that change periodically). If fixed expenses occur on a monthly basis, then record monthly. If your variable expenses also occur monthly, then record a minimum of 6-12 months' worth of payments and determine the average. To calculate a six-month average, add six months expenses and divide the total by six.

Expenses	Jan.	Feb.	Mar.	Apr.	May	June	Total	Avg
Electricity	50	65	51	42	37	55	300	50
Telephone	25	30	31	35	51	32	204	34

Rank each expense. Use numbers 1-10, with 10 being your most important. For example, housing and food should be 10's and movies and books may be 3's.

Your ***need ranking*** might look like this:

1. House	10
2. Food	10
3. Clothing	08

Your ***want ranking*** might look like this:

1. Eating out	10
2. Books	06
3. Movies	02

Balance your income with your expenses

Total Income (minus) - Goals (minus) - Fixed Expenses (needs)(minus)- Variable Expenses (needs) = Money available for fixed and variable wants & luxuries

Develop a Spending Plan

Allocate money from your income to each expense in order of ranking.

Enjoy a surplus, great! You're on your way to prosperity!

Correct a deficit, don't despair. You have several choices. Look for ways to increase your income. Evaluate what you have to offer. You can temporarily secure additional employment.

Look for ways to further reduce spending through debt reduction. Remember, the more debt you possess, the more and longer you spend money on interest payments. Re-negotiate payment terms with creditors.

Look for ways to spend more efficiently. (See spending.) "Trim some of the fat" from your wants. Remember, when you spend more money on your wants than you should, your needs become more pressing, causing stress.

Pray Although we live in a material realm, we have a Father in Heaven whose will influences the material realm. God specializes in helping those in seemingly helpless situations. He'll help you. In Psalm 37:25 David states, "I was young and now I am old, yet I have never seen the righteous forsaken or their children begging bread" (NIV). Be specific in your requests.

Adjust your plan to changes As you progress in life, your goals, income, and expenses will change. Your budget should change as well. Adjusting your budget to these changes ensures that you remain on track and keep moving toward your established financial destination.

Reap the Benefits of a Financial Plan

Control overspending Many people spend more than they earn. A budget will quickly reveal the aspects of your life where you're spending too much money. A budget will enable you to remain in control of your finances.

Track your expenditures Most people get into debt because they don't realize how much money they're spending. A budget provides an accurate record of expenditures. An unrecorded ATM withdrawal here and a credit card charge there can quickly land you in debt. The average American carries between 8 and 10 credit cards, each with an average balance of $1,900.00.

Organize your finances Organizing your finances is key to attaining and maintaining wealth. It helps prevent your money from slipping through the "cracks" without your knowledge.

Limit Debt If you don't want debt, don't borrow. If you don't want to go deeper into debt, don't borrow any more money. Armed with the knowledge of your spending habits, you can develop a budget and reverse your descent into debt. Ninety percent of personal bankruptcies result from credit card abuse.

Plan for surplus Following a budget will move your desire to save money from wishful thinking into a specific plan of action.

Prepare for emergencies Your car is going to require repairs one day. Do you have money set aside for that purpose? A budget helps you to anticipate unplanned expenditures that so often end up on a credit card.

Summary

Spending

Relative to the individual.

Amounts should be:

- Less for items
- More for journey (to financial stability/ independence)

Seeds for Overspending

Advertising

Expectations of Others

Love of Pleasure

Depression

Lack of Sound Financial Management

Tips on Spending Correctly

Spend based on what you value and what is really best for you.

Continue spending, change habits.

Spend with your financial plan in mind.

Chapter 6
Consumer Viewpoint: Debt

Debt is defined as something owed by one person to another or others, an obligation or liability to pay or return something.

The word "debt" causes anxiety and worry in many people. Debt is something no one wants after acquiring it, but people continually find new ways of adding debt daily through charge cards and making purchases with other types of consumer financing. It seems many people neither control their financial lives nor seek to do so.

Debt has always been a means of control. In every society where slavery existed, we found no rich slaves. There were some slaves who didn't experience the harsh treatment other slaves did, but they were slaves nonetheless. Debt stifles creativity. Debt can be such a debilitating experience that God instituted the year of Jubilee so that the poor among His people would be given an opportunity to begin anew. This Jubilee is a foreshadow of Christ's forgiveness, in that people could have been debtors all of their lives and during Jubilee would be forgiven of all debt to start anew. Debt takes people's focus away from their purpose. Debt therefore is a type of slavery - for as the Bible indicates, "the borrower is the slave of the lender" (Proverbs 22:7, RSV).

Types of Debt

There are two types of debt: financing debt and consumer debt.

Financing Debt is the use of credit to finance your goals. It's all right to finance your dreams of freedom (a business) and your acquisition of real assets with other people's money/property. The widow woman in 2 Kings 4:1-7 borrowed containers from her neighbors (to acquire assets).

Financing debt is future-oriented. The objective of financing debt is to earn money in the future exceeding the amount of money borrowed in the present.

Consumer Debt is the use of credit to finance your consumer purchases. Consumer debt keeps your financial focus on the past. The result of consumer debt is that the money repaid in the future will be more than the value of the original purchase. This debt consists primarily of credit card purchases. Credit cards may allow you to get what you want even when you aren't ready to handle it (the cost, which then becomes debt). This will add leanness to your soul (make you miserable). Why? Financially speaking, if consumer financing is considered, then the item is already unaffordable. By using consumer financing, people make an already unaffordable item even more expensive due to the addition of interest to the repayment of principal. As you engage in more transactions of this nature, eventually your finances will be unable to support the required interest payments.

When it comes to debt, we must not allow our desires alone to guide us. Being led by desires can be the worst scenario in which a debtor/slave can be. You can waste your life wanting something else not in God's time. If the debtor is allowed a few pleasures (from credit cards), when someone teaches him a higher way (frees or redeems him) and he encounters difficulty during his new-found freedom (adhering to budget/responsible spending), then he will long for slavery (debt) because of the loss of a little pleasure (Numbers 11:4-6, 18-20).

Interest Rates and Their Effect on You

Home equity loans, automobile loans, and credit cards all represent the use of someone else's money to acquire what we want. The price we pay for using someone else's money is called interest. Interest rates in the aforementioned bank products are influenced greatly by the Prime Rate. The Prime Rate is the rate charged to their most creditworthy customers(posted by at least 75% of the 30 largest U.S. banks surveyed by the Wall Street Journal). The Prime Rate, in addition to a mark up imposed by individual banks based on the risk of the transaction/borrower, influences your credit card, and other loan rates. In addition to the standard mark up or "margin" rate, credit card issuers have established a "universal default interest rate". You could be subject to a default rate as high as 30%. This rate comes into play whenever the following occurs: a late payment is made to any of your creditors, when your account is over the credit balance limit, or when you have missed payments. Ask your credit card issuer or read the fine print of your credit card agreement to find out in what cases (if any) this default rate would apply to you.

Credit Card Advantages/Disadvantages

As with anything, if used properly or improperly, credit can be a blessing or a curse. Here are a few pros and cons of using a credit card.

Advantages using a credit card:

a) Provides consumer protection from theft and damaged goods.
b) Provides an alternative to carrying cash.
c) Assists you in building a credit history.

Disadvantages using a credit card:

a) Can increase the actual cost of an item through the addition of interest.
b) Creates a belief that credit is like cash.
c) Encourages overspending.

Results of Debt/Slavery

To gain a greater understanding of the effects of debt, let's look more closely at five characteristics shared by debt and slavery.

1) Both can prevent you from doing what you want with what you have (living in freedom).
2) Both can lead to poor health.
3) Both can breed anxiety, despair, depression, distress, bitterness, worry, and discontent.

4) Both can give someone else power over you and maintain that power until you take steps to remove it.
5) Both can seek to force you into hard labor.

Inability to Do What You Want (Live in Freedom) What's preventing you from doing what you would like to do, or going where you would like to go? Debt. You feel you can't do anything or go anywhere until you pay off old debts. Indebtedness causes you to take on (accept) harder work. Why? The lender will require it for the income to pay him. This prevents you from thinking about or attending to what you really want to do with your money. (See Exodus 5:9.)

Poor Heath Negative emotions affect your mind for the worse, and whatever affects your mind manifests itself in your body, because the mind and body are two sides of the same coin. High blood pressure, cardiovascular problems, arthritis, etc., are sometimes physical manifestations of the effect of negative emotions on the mind.

Negative Emotions You feel miserable when you can't do what you want. You worry when your debt exceeds what you have. You feel depressed and in despair when you feel there's no way out.

Someone Else in Power Over You When you are in debt to someone, your lender has power over you.

Labor for Another's Profit Does it not seem that the harder you work, the richer your lenders become? The nature of debt causes one (the lender) to increase and the other (the debtor) to decrease.

Modern System of Debt

President George W. Bush's administration rewrote the bankruptcy laws, making it more difficult for people to file bankruptcy. This change and similar changes are being made mainly to protect credit card issuers, who hold obligations valued at millions of dollars. This money is due from average Americans, the majority of whom earn around $20,000 per year but are tens of thousands of dollars in debt!

Contributing to the modern system of debt is an Income Tax structure designed to benefit from increase and promote government control, i.e., "the more you make, the more they take."

The modern system of debt is based on this theory of collaboration between creditors (mainly credit card issuers) and government. When credit cards were introduced, the interest was deductible on income taxes. Why? Because the government was encouraging people to stimulate production (and employment) by increasing demand. The resulting interest on debt was deductible from taxes. Once the use of credit cards increased dramatically, the incentive of tax deduction was no longer needed, and the modern system of debt was born: those in debt work; the more you work, the more money you make; the more you make, the more is available for the government to tax. Sounds unbelievable? Then see the example below:

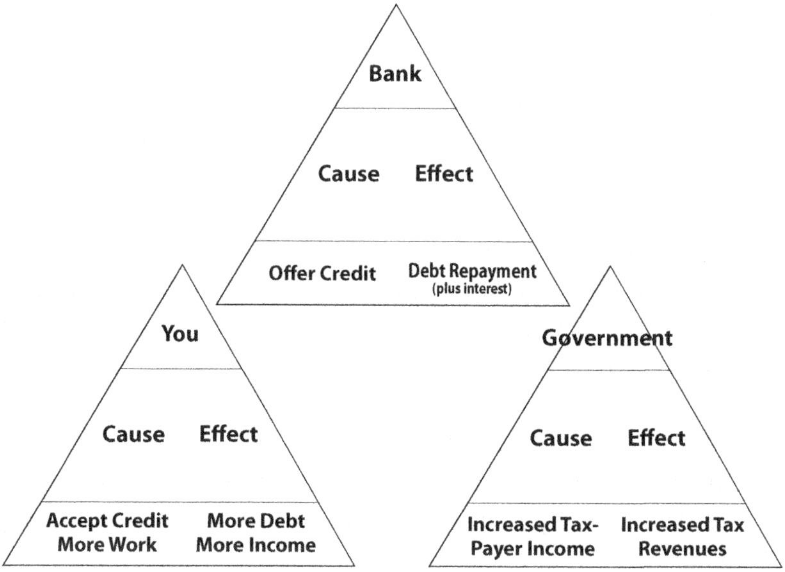

Cause: Offer/Accept Credit
Effect on Credit Issuer: New Debtor, potential to earn more money
Effect on You: More Debt

Cause: More Work
Effect on You: More income, stress, less free time
Effect on Government: More Income Tax Revenue

In this scenario, only the government and credit issuers benefit.

Biblical System of Debt

In the biblical system, debtors were treated like people. They were able to maintain their dignity without being made to feel as if they were failures. The Lord's Year of Release (Deuteronomy 15) afforded an opportunity for starting over regardless of the amount of debt. The law required every creditor that lent to his neighbor to release him from the debt and not exact payment from the lender's neighbor or brother, because the year was called The Lord's Release.

The rich were not able to prosper to the detriment of those in poverty. God made provisions for the poor. If people were sold into slavery, they were to be paid so that they might prosper at the end of their servitude.

In today's world, your creditors wouldn't offer you a job; they would seek to take everything you had. In the biblical system the creditors were not harsh to the debtors because the creditors realized that they themselves were in debt to God.

There was a point when the biblical system was disrupted and the rich enslaved the poor for profit and didn't pay them. This created a perpetual system of poverty. The rich hoarded the money for themselves. Sound familiar?

The biblical system was originally designed so that the rich would profit by helping others - hiring them to work in their fields and then receiving the Blessing of God (Deuteronomy 15). The more workers, the more the rich could plant; the more they planted, the greater the yield; the greater the yield, the more money could be made.

Difference between Modern and Biblical Systems of Debt

The modern system is designed for others to profit by placing you and keeping you in debt. The biblical system is designed for others to profit by helping their brothers (you) and hiring other people as workers. As the differences between the Modern and Biblical Systems of Debt became more apparent, debtors (more easily avoided) or did not allow creditors to profit from their consumer debt.

Causes of Consumer Debt

Consumer debt may result from any, or a combination, of several factors:

a) Lack of financial management
b) Lack of saving
c) Lack of understanding of debt
d) Lack of willingness to delay gratification

Lack of Financial Management There are many of you who may be totally unaware of the state of your finances. Slaves to debt neither knew nor were concerned much about their finances. So financial management was/is not something widely learned among families. As a result, many people have been convinced that acquiring things is more important than saving money. This explains why people are willing to pay credit card interest to purchase a consumer item. That lack of education has been passed on from generation to generation, resulting in many people excessively purchasing things (cars, clothes, jewelry, etc.) they currently can't financially afford.

Lack of Saving A lack of saving can cause debt. God never promised that every day would be sunny. There may be times when famine (as during Joseph's time, Genesis 41) or medical emergency (as with the woman with the issue of blood, Mark 5:25-34; Luke 8:43-48) can cause debt. Joseph's creative use of saving during prosperous times caused him to prosper even during lean times. Remember, although the general populace was unaware of the pending famine, they still had the opportunity to save as Joseph did. Yet the general populace didn't save, and they were forced into poverty/debt.

Lack of Understanding of Debt We live in a time in which we can acquire most anything we want by credit. Unfortunately, most don't understand how credit and interest work. Certainly, credit offers an opportunity to possess things many ordinarily couldn't afford to have. However, that accessibility comes with a price which we know as interest.

Interest simply means the extra amount paid, above what is borrowed, for the use of credit. Credit purchases extend many beyond their financial means, and interest adds to the balance owed. Because most people couldn't afford the item anyway and because the balance due is paid back over time, the interest is given the opportunity to increase the creditors' investment over time at the borrower's (your) expense.

Lack of Willingness to Delay Gratification Do you know someone who always has nice clothes or other trinkets, who is always testifying how the Lord provides, but who seeks to borrow money from you or others to pay the rent, mortgage, or some other expected expense later on in the month? Then, that person's undisciplined desires (unwillingness to wait and save for what he or she desires) are leading him or her into debt. Don't lend him any money. Why should your financial goals and plans suffer from that person's lack of wisdom? As the scripture indicates, "He that loveth pleasure shall be a poor man" (Proverbs 21:17, KJV).

Ways to Stay in Debt

Use Credit Unwisely It's your unwise use of the lender's (master's) product - credit - which gives the lender the ability to provide you a few simple pleasures of wealth at your own expense. Indulgence in those pleasures helps you to forget temporarily the perceived harshness of your reality. Indulgence can also contribute to your fantasy, creating an unending circle of servitude.

Ignore Debt As with slavery, you can seek to escape debt by running away (ignoring it). If you are caught, you will pay the consequences. Those consequences include judgments, poor credit scores, etc., that negatively affect your financial picture.

Expect to be in Debt Some of you are indifferent about debt because you don't see past today financially. The inability to see past the item you want to purchase limits your financial prosperity. Is your goal to satisfy present desire with no regard for tomorrow? If you answered yes, then perhaps your upbringing may have contributed to this thinking pattern. I'm sure there are a number of you reading this book who were born into a family of debtors; your parents lived in debt . . . so forth and so on. Does this sound like you? Are you convinced that you are destined to a life of debt, so much so that being in debt doesn't disturb you? Have you "numbed" yourself with indifference to debt, with hopes of coping with the condition rather than seeking treatment? As with any negative condition, even if you don't feel it, if left untreated it could have catastrophic results. You must take the proper steps to remove the debt.

Three Common Errors that Don't Free You from Debt

My experience has helped me to identify three common errors that don't free you from debt:

1) Receiving more money
2) Overworking for money
3) Taking out consolidation loans

Receiving More Money A windfall of money doesn't guarantee freedom from debt. Lack of money usually isn't the cause of debt, financial ignorance is. So if financial ignorance is usually the cause of debt: then financial knowledge will be required to eliminate debt. Having an abundance of money would only make the situation worse.

So often, I encounter people who say they are praying for money to satisfy debts, but they have never attended financial seminars, mine or anyone else's. By praying for money they are asking God to address the symptom, not the cause. I'm sure that you have heard stories of individuals who have come into large sums of money. Constructive thinking would have them eliminate past debts and live happily ever after, but studies prove that they don't. They acquire more debt, so much so that it exceeds the amount of money they acquired!

The story of the Children of Israel tells us that although you can give a poor person money to make him rich, if his thought pattern hasn't been changed, then riches won't benefit him. Although the Children of Israel were millionaires, they still behaved (complained) like oppressed people.

Overworking for Money Consistently working harder for money keeps you from concentrating on developing the gift that will truly prosper you. Early in our marriage my wife wanted to get a part-time job to earn extra personal money and to liquidate some debts. I suggested that she shouldn't take on this additional work solely for money. Here's why: I told her that for the amount of time required to travel to the extra job, the vehicle expense, the additional stress, the increase in taxes (remember "the more you make, the more they take"), and the low pay, I could see no discernible benefit to her. The job wasn't something she enjoyed, nor was it something related to her goals, objectives, and present training. It would only keep her from working on the gift in which she is truly talented, which is writing. As any serious writer knows, writing requires a serious amount of time and dedication. Working 18-24 additional hours per week would seriously hamper her writing and future success. Which one is more beneficial - working harder on any job for short-term cash or working on your talent for long-term prosperity? She decided to heed my advice, and the things she wanted to buy she has since purchased debt-free, and the debt she wanted to liquidate was paid without hampering her long-term success.

Acquiring Consolidation Loans Consolidation loans shouldn't be considered before developing a solid understanding of how debt works and how to eliminate it. When you consolidate your debt, you're trading short-term obligations for long-term debt. While it's possible your monthly payments could be lower, the total amount of debt you owe increases. If a detailed plan isn't in place, you could find yourself in more debt than before.

Studies prove that a deterioration in financial condition affects a significant number of people who consolidate their debt. By not addressing the cause of debt (financial ignorance) or at the very least stopping their credit card spending, people eventually allow their habits to pull them into an even worse financial position.

Remember, you don't want just to be given respite and to remain enslaved (in debt). Your ultimate goal is to be free. And not attempting to do the impossible by borrowing your way out of debt is a step in the right direction. Further immersing yourself into a system designed to keep you and everyone else in debt is not wise. Basically, all consolidation does is lighten your payments (workload) and increase the length of servitude to the lender. Only the designers of the modern system of debt would design a system which projects the illusion that debt can be used to get out of debt.

Three Steps toward Freedom from Debt

My experience has led me to identify three steps toward freedom from debt. They are:

1) Acquire Knowledge
2) Make Sound Choices
3) Act

Acquire Knowledge The first step to being free from debt is to acquire something slaves neither have nor believe they can possess: education/knowledge.

You can get education/knowledge about debt, what puts you in debt, what takes you out of debt, and whom to contact if debt is overwhelming. Read books, listen to tapes, and attend seminars: do anything that will increase your financial awareness. If financial matters aren't your cup of tea, then hire someone who has the knowledge to help you. Possession of or access to knowledge enables you to recognize good choices.

Make Sound Choices Choices enable you to decide on a course of action and follow it through. Knowledge and choices work together, because without knowledge you wouldn't be aware of the choices available to you and how to take full advantage of them. You must make the choice to be free (set goals, save, budget, etc.), because the slave master (person/entity to whom you are in debt) wants you to remain in debt and work to make him rich. "The rich rules over the poor, and the borrower is servant to the lender" (Proverbs 22:7, NKJV).

When I started my consulting practice, I applied for and received a credit card, which I used to finance start-up expenses. After I used the card, I always paid anywhere from five to ten times the minimum payment amount as my monthly payment. After three months I received an "automatic" increase in my credit limit. Why did my credit card company give me that increase? They said it was because I was a "good" customer. Good customer? If I were such a "good" customer, then why not automatically decrease my interest rate, or credit my account, etc.?

No, to them a "good" customer is someone who charges, pays more than the minimum, but has a revolving balance. They believed that if I could make such large monthly payments, they could increase my credit limit with the goal of encouraging me to spend more using the card while maintaining the same payment frequency. Note I didn't say amount. They didn't care if I ever paid off the card. They actually preferred that I made the minimum payment. Their goal is to use me as a means of cash flow for their business, at my expense, for as long as possible. Hence they propose minuscule minimum monthly payments.

Act Without purposeful action your financial life becomes like that of people who have given up and are praying to win the lottery. In the New Testament James said, "Faith by itself, if it does not have works, is dead" (James 2:17, NKJV). So you can say all you want that you have faith that God will help you get out of debt. Without action we know that your "lip faith" is alive, but your "do faith" is dead.

For a financial miracle it will take some talking (prayer) and some doing, not talking and sitting. What type of action is required? Use the knowledge you have acquired, or the help you've hired, to make sound choices, which will take you where you want to go financially. Purposeful action is the vehicle by which we travel to our destination. In this case, the destination is freedom from debt.

Five Steps to Remove Debt

A better way than perpetuating, ignoring, or enduring debt is to get out of debt, doing it piece by piece if no one is able to redeem you outright. To begin you must view your debts with the objective of eliminating as many as possible as soon as possible.

The principle Jesus said is truly reflected here: a house divided against itself won't stand. The same principle applies to debt. Only that which is opposed to debt will get you out of debt. Those things are saving, wise spending, giving, investing, and paying bills out of your substance.

Make plans, set objectives and goals. Is being debt-free your goal? If so, then you must think about being debt-free every day. When achieving freedom from debt became my goal, I started seeing opportunities I had missed or had been too afraid to attempt. Working to remove my debts is active thought. Active thought is thinking about the solution, not the problem. Active thought leads to action.

What has thinking about the debt gotten you? Worry, anxiety, and fear. Why? Inactive thought it keeps you focused on the problem. The focus of inactive thinking is always on the problem, not the solution. Inactive thinking presents a hopeless situation. "Oh poor me, I can't do anything about my debt." Every situation is crying out for a solution, but if you are thinking about the problem (being in debt) and not the solution (how to get out of debt), then your inactive thinking will keep you right in debt.

Debtors who were resigned to remaining debtors usually remained debtors their entire lives, even if they experienced a financial windfall such as an inheritance or lottery winning. The debtor who desires freedom (being debt-free) thinks and sings about being free every day. It is this constant thinking of being free which leads you to realize and take advantage of opportunities to be free.

Using the following steps helped me to rid myself of several thousand dollars of consumer debt.

Desire to eliminate debt Sometimes your financial miracle starts with your seeking to repay your debts. That's what happened to the widow in 2 Kings 4:1-7. Although the main focus of this passage of scripture is God's miracle of provision, if the widow woman had not sought to pay her bills, then perhaps God would not have provided such a great financial miracle. Hmm . . . get the picture? Seek to pay your debts.

Analyze your debts In analyzing your debts you want to make a list of whom you owe, phone number/address, the amounts owed, the monthly minimum payments, and interest rate. This gives you a look at the big picture and is a sign of responsibility.

Arrange debts Next, arrange your debts in descending order from largest to smallest amount owed. Prioritize based on your desire to free up as much cash as possible as soon as possible.

For example, a borrower has three debts:

a) $1000.00 Balance	19% interest	$165.00/month payments.
b) $ 500.00 Balance	20% interest	$ 50.00/month payments.
c) $ 250.00 Balance	10% interest	$ 25.00/month payments.

Some credit counselors would say pay extra money to eliminate the high interest debts first, which is good if saving on interest is your objective. If you want to prosper and relieve stress, you first need to increase cash flow. Cash flow represents the amount of money flowing into your possession, usually measured on a monthly basis. Paying off the smallest debt first, regardless of interest, increases cash flow. Then proceed to the next smallest debt. Your prosperity is determined not by how much interest you save per se, but by how much more cash than expenses you have flowing in. By paying off your smallest debt first without regard to interest rates, you free cash more quickly. Remember, the amount of money you free up monthly is the measure of your freedom and ability to prosper.

Set Payoff Date Set a date by which you want to be free of this entire debt. Be realistic, and base your payoff date on your current monthly earnings. If your present income is not enough and/or your credit score is suffering, you may consider reducing your debt by:

a) Contacting creditors and asking for interest rate reduction (thereby decreasing total amount owed), offering to settle the account by paying 60-80% of the current balance using your savings, and/or requesting a temporary reduction in minimum monthly payment,

b) Seeking to reduce spending, or

c) Seeking temporary employment.

Allocate money for monthly payments This allocation is based on your budget. Use available money to make payments. But some of you may say you are still not able to allocate enough money for payments. Then you will have to adjust your spending.

I remember years ago living in a very small studio apartment, and funds were tight. On Friday nights after work, I would order a pizza and relax. This happened every Friday. When getting out of debt became my goal and I realized how truly limited my funds were, I noticed that I was spending about $10 per week on pizza. That amounted to about $520 per year!! Could you imagine? If I continued at that rate for five years, I would spend an amount that would have paid off about 1/3 of my debts!!

What is your spending like? Are you spending money on something less important than getting out of debt? Is your spending out of control? Is acquiring things more pleasurable or important than reaching your financial destination (goals)? If presented with a choice of buying the new dress (or the new suit) - or using that money to pay debts - which would you choose?

Using Savings to Pay Debt

As stated earlier, savings can and should be used to reduce debt - to a point - and ideally, if the debt reduction frees up additional income. Remember, a portion of your savings (seed) should be used as an emergency reserve. If you decide to use savings to pay a creditor, you must balance the amounts you use toward reducing a debt, so that you have some left to plant (give/invest) that you may prosper.

Importance of Paying Bills

Part of being a good steward is paying your bills. Paying your bills on time and consistently demonstrates responsibility to your lender. God can prosper those who handle things responsibly. In the secular world, your stewardship is measured by your credit or FICO score. This score is a measure of your credit-rating calculated from data contained in your credit report. There are five categories of credit data that influence your credit score in varying degrees:

·Outstanding Balance	30%
·Payment History	35%
·Length of Credit History	15%
·New Credit	10%
·Type of Credit Use	10%

As you can see, your payment history accounts for 35% of your credit score. Most lenders base their credit decisions on your score. Generally, the higher your score, the more likely a lender is to approve your loan and the more likely you may qualify for a lower interest rate when you borrow, which highlights the importance of paying your bills

When borrowing, there are some things of which you must be aware. First, you will pay back more money than you borrowed. Secondly, as the scripture indicates in Proverbs 22:7b, “the borrower is servant to the lender” (NKJV). That means that by receiving money from the lender you become subject to certain terms, such as interest rate and payment frequency, that are required by the lender. Third, the way you handle your responsibility as a borrower is reflected on your credit report, which is used by future lenders to aid in determining if you will repay your loans. Lastly, although this scripture is not frequently quoted, the scripture indicates, “The wicked borrows and does not repay” (Psalms 37:21, NKJV). Personally, I have lent money to people who intially promised to repay, but didn’t. Their lack of response and poor character were very disappointing.

Before I continue, let me tell you that I’m not talking about those who may have felt they had no recourse but to file bankruptcy due to inability to repay overwhelming debt. I’m talking about the people who have the money to buy the things they want but are not seeking to repay those who lent money to them.

As a believer, you must repay your debts: if you do not, the Bible counts you among the wicked. The belief that being a Christian excuses you from repaying debt is false. To pay someone you owe is just and fair. God’s sense of fairness and justice demands it. If that were not the case, then Jesus would not have been required to give His life to satisfy our debt to God. There are many in the Body of Christ who owe one another but have not treated the lender fairly. God is the God of the lender too, and if the lender cries out to God against you, your non-payment becomes sin to you! Unpaid debt has caused friendships to dissolve and enmity between brethren, as all sin does.

Summary

Characteristics of a Lending Transaction
You will pay back more than you borrowed.
You will be subject to the lender.
Your fulfillment or non-fulfillment of the agreement affects future credit.

Characteristics of a Consolidation Loan
You trade short-term higher payments on debt for long-term debt with lower payments.
Monthly payments are lower, but the total amount you owe increases.

Five Steps to Remove Debt
Desire to eliminate debt
Analyze your debts
Arrange debts
Set payoff date
Allocate money for monthly payments

Chapter 7
Provider Viewpoint: Giving

Giving represents money given to a charitable work or person in need. God is a giver. He has given us many different things including the opportunity to be givers ourselves and meet the needs of others. The only requirements are that we acknowledge the fact that God actually owns everything, and that we use His wealth wisely to take care of our needs and to bless others, and then He will bless us. Before He can bless us, we must first demonstrate that we can handle wealth by meeting God's requirement of tithing.

Tithing is evidence that you realize that everything you "own" is actually God's and that you honor Him by giving 10% of your income back to Him. God blesses those who are faithful concerning their finances. This is consistent with the principle of faithfulness in little, then rulership in much (Matthew 25:23).

My purpose in this section is to highlight the blessing and importance of tithing. If you are familiar with tithing and are unsure whether this is something required in the Old Testament Law but not applicable under New Testament Grace, please seek teaching from other sources. Teaching from other sources is also suggested if you are confused about whether you should tithe on net or gross income. My sole contribution to this discussion would be, "Is the difference between one-tenth of your gross income and one-tenth of your net income enough to cause you to cry, 'Poverty!'?" Then I would encourage you to examine how you handle finances (and continue reading). If you want to prosper, stop fighting the inclination to honor your father God by giving your tithe.

Your energies would be better spent fighting your "uncle" who takes 2-5 times that amount with no return to you. You guessed it, Uncle Sam!! Taxes take away from you but do not (by nature) cause you, or put you in a position, to increase. The tithe, on the other hand, ushers you to the doors of opportunity to increase. So what am I saying? I'm saying, pay your taxes. I would suggest that you use every legal means for tax deductions available to you. I'm also saying give your tithe. Even if funds are tight, let God present an opportunity for you to increase.

Prior to completing this book, I encountered an emergency financial situation that would have called for me to nearly liquidate my savings. To say I was worried was an understatement. So I began to pray for money, and God told me to give $500 to my church!! Now, your eyes aren't playing tricks on you, He told me to give $500, when my funds were very tight. After giving the money I felt a release in my spirit that I hadn't felt before. I was at peace. Not only was I at peace, but the money I needed arrived in the nick of time.

I'm sure that some of you may know someone who "appears" to be increasing and not giving the tithe. My suggestion would be, let your focus be on your relationship with God and the additional benefits tithing brings to you. It has been my experience that tithing provides opportunities for increase. When I moved to my current city, I was several thousands of dollars in debt. I had no car and no home. Shortly before my arrival in my new city, I adopted the principle of tithing. To say that tithing (along with wise financial planning) contributed greatly to turning my financial picture around would be an understatement. Within three years I received a promotion, nearly doubled my income, paid off all of my past debts, purchased a car and a home, and participated in several investment opportunities.

There are many different ways to increase. Some of the benefits that tithing include: Supernatural provision of opportunities for increase, Presence of God, Positive effect on health, Protection from Satan, and Recognition (People everywhere will call you Blessed).

Types of Giving

Costless Giving is turning over possession or control of something to someone without either cost to the recipient or exchange of goods or services.

Faith Promise Giving involves identifying the gift you want to receive and promising, before you receive it, to give it.

Each type of gift shares one or more of the following characteristics:

a) The gift must first be offered from a willing mind.
b) The gift must be measurable.
c) The gift gives life to others and self.
d) The gift must be given cheerfully.
e) The gift must be in accordance with what you have.
f) The gift may be given on the spur of the moment.
g) The gift must be given unselfishly.

Costless Giving Costless Giving planned in advance is a sign of good financial management. Costless giving in advance is intended not to bless others at your expense, but to share your abundance resulting from sound financial management and increase (2 Corinthians 9:8). The Bible states that costless gifts should be given to the church (Deuteronomy 12:5-6) and to the underprivileged - the poor, aliens, orphans, and widows (Deuteronomy 24:19-21; Psalm 146:9; Proverbs 28:27).

Costless giving may be done bountifully or sparingly. When talking about giving bountifully or sparingly, I'm referring to not just to the amount or size of the gift, but the spirit by which it is given. Your heart and spirit must be in alignment to reap. This principle is found in 2 Corinthians 9:6-8:

v6 "But this I say: He who sows sparingly will also reap sparingly, and he who sows bountifully will also reap bountifully.
v7 "So let each one give as he purposes in his heart, not grudgingly or of necessity; for God loves a cheerful giver" (NKJV).

V8 "And God is able to make all grace abound toward you, that you, always having all sufficiency in all things, may have an abundance for every good work." (NKJV).

I have encountered people who feel that they have given much but have not reaped in proportion to the size of their gifts. After a little investigation, I learn that they have usually given improperly: they may have given the gift, but they didn't give freely. They held on to it in their hearts and/or gave grudgingly. If you give sparingly, then you reap in the same manner. At face value this scripture says that the more you give the more you receive. Man's viewpoint is on the size of the gift, while God's viewpoint is not limited to the size of the gift. Mark 12:41-44 (NKJV) provides an excellent example of this.

v41 Now Jesus sat opposite the treasury and saw how the people put money into the treasury. And many who were rich put in much.
v42 Then one poor widow came and threw in two mites, which make a quadrans.
v43 So He called His disciples to Himself and said to them, "Assuredly, I say to you that this poor widow has put in more than all those who have given to the treasury;
v44 "for they all put in out of their abundance, but she out of her poverty put in all that she had, her whole livelihood."

The fundamental principle behind giving is the provision of something by one party to another with or without cost. Giving increases you because it is undergirded by this principle, "Give, and it shall be given unto you" (Luke 6:38). These principles offer proof that being a true provider can lift you out of poverty or ensure continued prosperity. Other characteristics of costless giving are: The individuals you provide for are not able to pay. God steps in and pays you for your services many-fold, because when you provide for God, He not only pays (meets your needs), He multiplies the payment above and beyond what you can imagine. Giving is a spiritual act. Your actual gift begins in the spirit. The condition of your heart affects how you give and your return, regardless of the amount given. Costless giving is an act of Worship. The scripture says that the way you handle your finances is an indication of the way you would and do handle spiritual things. Why? Because giving literally comes from the heart. The status of your heart at the moment of the gift determines whether you receive a bountiful or sparing return. Giving enables us to participate with God in meeting the needs of others. He actually owns everything, but He allows us to use His money to bless others. Giving places you in a position to receive. God gave His only son to die for the sins of the world, so that He could receive us as His children (John 3:16).

As I indicated previously, giving can be planned in advance. You must use money wisely during that period to ensure you have the right amount of money at the time you propose to give it, and that it will not put a strain on you, causing you to give it reluctantly. Giving must be unselfish. Each person should give what he has decided in his heart to give, not reluctantly or under compulsion (2 Corinthians 9:7).

Faith-Promise Giving As mentioned earlier, Faith-Promise Giving involves the identification of the gift you want to receive and the promise, before you receive it, to give it. Normally, an individual participating in this type of giving is asking God to provide something from an unexpected source. Upon receipt, all is given to God. In the book of 1 Samuel, Samuel's mother, Hannah, was barren and without child. Hannah went to the tabernacle and prayed for a son, and she promised to give him to the Lord. Once Hannah gave Samuel to the Lord, as promised, she was blessed with three additional sons and two daughters. As the story of Hannah bears witness, faith-promise giving is actually the seed that God uses to multiply, not the seed for your consumption. I believe that God used this story as an example to show how powerful Faith-Promise Giving is. Even if you have nothing and promise to give when you receive what you are asking for, He can still multiply it in advance of your receiving it.

The Giving Cycle

Another means I believe God provides His people for increase is the Giving Cycle. The scriptures teach that money is considered seed. The scriptures admonish us to plant (give) as a farmer would plant (sow). The farmer plants as much as possible because he realizes that one seed can yield manifold increases.

So, give as much as possible during the right time and plant in good ground. Once planted, seeds must be nurtured as a farmer nurtures his seed. To properly benefit from this principle for generating wealth, you must follow and adhere to the following steps:

1.) Fertilize Ground (start with the church),
2.) Plant Seeds (make Gifts/Offerings),
3.) Dig out Weeds (deny Self) and,
4.) Feed/Water (study the Word of God).

Fertilize Ground Any farmer will tell you that the type of ground in which you plant your seed determines the success and size of the harvest. Luke 8:5-8 tells us that during the planting process our seeds can be scattered on the wayside (path), on rocks, in the midst of weeds, or in good ground. Before planting any seed, the wise farmer would ensure proper development of the seed by fertilizing the ground first to make it good. Fertilizing to ensure good ground is represented by tithing to the Christ-centered church. These churches are identified by the return on your fertilization, i.e., the increase in souls won, hungry people fed, homeless people housed, and sound management of the money they receive, for example. We, as children of God, should primarily support our local churches as evidenced in the principle noted in 1 Timothy 5:4 which encourages children and grandchildren to first learn to show piety at home (loyalty and devotion to family and ministry around you). Remember the tithe is used to support God's house (church) that the windows of heaven may be opened over you. By choosing to fertilize these types of ministries (God's Ground) first, you ensure fertility for other charitable ground in which you plant your seeds, whether that be for disease research, programs to feed the hungry, protection of nature, or some other cause.

As I mentioned earlier, not everyone tithes. By not tithing, I believe that non-tithers miss out on the guarantee of fertile ground that tithing brings. Those who are "prospering" would disagree with me, because they have reaped some increase. The prosperity they have reaped is due not to proper planting but to God's grace, which can cause people to increase even though they may not be aware of or acknowledge the tithe. Still, no matter how much they have received, it can't compare to what they could have reaped had they consistently fertilized their ground. What they don't know is that many people plant their seeds in the ground but have not guaranteed that the ground is fertile. Your planting process then becomes hit or miss. To date, every investment I have made has either increased or led me to another opportunity that brought more than I thought I might have lost in the previous opportunity.

Plant Seeds Although I believe that the church is the most "fertile soil" for your money (offering), because the effects are eternal, there are numerous charities which are very "mission-minded," but are not directly associated with the church, that can provide fertile ground for a portion of your seed. Some of these programs feed the hungry, clothe the naked, give shelter to the homeless, research cures for diseases, provide scholarships, provide nursing home care, and accomplish many other mission-minded services for the greater good of humanity. I know that some people may feel that this thought is too radical, and that all of your offerings should be given to the church. If that is your belief, then I don't dispute you or encourage you to do otherwise, but if you take a closer look at Malachi 3:10, God says, "Bring all the tithes into the storehouse, that there may be food in My house" (NKJV). He didn't say bring all the tithes and offerings. I sincerely believe that God would have said bring all of the tithes and offerings into the storehouse if He required His people to give all of their gifts to the church.

As I mentioned earlier, there are people around you in need who can benefit from what you have. For example, my mother was in a situation where I could assist financially with the down payment to purchase her home. Could I morally say that I couldn't offer any money to her, because I had to offer it all to the church? Had I done that, I feel that I would have been in direct opposition to the principle Jesus noted in Mark 7:9-13:

v9 He said to them, "All too well you reject the commandment of God, that you may keep your tradition.
v10 "For Moses said, 'Honor your father and your mother'; and, 'He who curses father or mother, let him be put to death.'
v11 "But you say, 'If a man says to his father or mother, "Whatever profit you might have received from me is Corban"–' (that is a gift to God [church]),
v12 "then you no longer let him do anything for his father or his mother,
v13 "making the word of God of no effect through your tradition which you have handed down. And many such things you do" (NKJV).

I believe not only that God is pleased with such use of an offering (as I did with my mother), but that giving to people in need (the beggar on the street, parents in need, etc.) and other mission-minded organizations helps produce a financial harvest as part of the giving cycle.

Dig out Weeds As in the physical realm, the only things that can hinder the growth of your spiritual seeds are weeds. In the spiritual realm no weeds exist naturally in good ground. We bring the weeds to the good ground (church). Lack of belief, which is unrighteousness and sin, etc., is a weed that we bring to our good ground. To receive we must believe that receiving is a direct result of giving. For unhindered growth we must remove those weeds from the farming process. The answer to eliminating the weeds is found in 1 John 1:9, "If we confess our sins, He is faithful and just to forgive us our sins and to cleanse us from all unrighteousness" (NKJV).

Feed/Water Just like weeds flow through you to your seeds, so too does food/water flow through you to your seed. This food/water is talked about in Hebrews 5:12-13. The Word of God-when spoken from our mouths-becomes nourishment for our seeds. Examples of such words are, "Give and it shall be given unto you," or phrases similar to what I say to myself when I give: "I freely give this gift from my heart, and more shall be given to me." Our words are but an extension of our thoughts. And as the scriptures say, "As [a man] thinketh, so is he" (Prov. 23:7).

This principle not only applies to our mental state, but assists us in creating or arranging conditions that reflect our thoughts.

Claiming our Prosperity

Another way God blesses is when you claim existing property in the name of Jesus. I'm sure some of you may be saying that you have been claiming in Jesus' name since He left for Heaven and have yet to receive your prosperity.

One fact about claiming property is the realization that someone else has it and it must be transferred from him or her by God - to be given to you. The story of Joshua provides an example.

Joshua was the God-ordained leader to succeed Moses, with instructions to lead the children of Israel into the Promised Land. The Promised Land was being transferred from the wicked inhabitants of the land to those who were the chosen people of God. Though this is the first time this principle appears, it is not the only time it is mentioned. It is mentioned again in Proverbs 13:22b, "the wealth of the sinner is laid up for the just" (KJV). Since this is God's principle of Wealth Transfer, there are certain things that must be followed for the principle to work: worship, praise, and obedience.

This principle of wealth transferred from the wicked to the just first appeared in the book of Joshua. Before Joshua could take possession of the Promised Land, there were some things that had to be done. Joshua 5:13-15 picks up the story right before the Israelites were to embark on their first battle to claim their Land.

v13 "And it came to pass, when Joshua was by Jericho, that he lifted up his eyes and looked, and behold, a Man stood opposite him with His sword drawn in His hand. And Joshua went to Him and said to Him, "Are You for us or for our adversaries?""

v14 So He said, "No, but as Commander of the army of the Lord I have now come." And Joshua fell on his face to the earth and worshiped, and said to Him, "What does my Lord say to His servant?"
v15 Then the Commander of the Lord's army said to Joshua, "Take your sandal off your foot, for the place where you stand is holy" (NKJV).

Before the first battle, Joshua worshiped the Lord. By worshiping the Lord before the battle, you give Him the reverence and preeminence He deserves. This worship humbles you before God, enabling Him to be God in your situation and lead you to victory.

Prior to the battle of Jericho, the Lord gave the following instructions to the humble Joshua in Joshua 6:3-5.

v3 "You shall march around the city, all you men of war; you shall go all around the city once. This you shall do six days.
v4 "And seven priests shall bear seven trumpets of rams' horns before the ark. But the seventh day you shall march around the city seven times, and the priests shall blow the trumpets.
v5 "It shall come to pass, when they make a long blast with the ram's horn, and when you hear the sound of the trumpet, that all the people shall shout with a great shout; then the wall of the city will fall down flat. And the people shall go up every man straight before him" (NKJV).

Here Joshua learns that the Lord is to be praised before the victory. It's this praise to the Lord that guarantees victory.

Joshua and the Israelites have experienced victory at Jericho, and nothing can stop them from claiming their continued victory, because God has shown them the key, right? As the children of Israel learned, this is regrettably wrong. After the great victory at Jericho, the children of Israel assumed the victory at Ai would be easy. Unknown to them at the time, one of their own committed an act which prevented them from having further claim to the property which was theirs as a gift from God. That act was an act of disobedience.

In Joshua 7:11-12 & 21 we discover that one of the children of Israel, Achan, disobeyed God by taking gold and silver away from Jericho.

v11 "Israel has sinned, and they have also transgressed My covenant which I commanded them. For they have even taken some of the accursed things, and have both stolen and deceived; and they have also put it among their own stuff.
v12 "Therefore the children of Israel could not stand before their enemies, but turned their backs before their enemies, because they have become doomed to destruction. Neither will I be with you anymore, unless you destroy the accursed from among you" (NKJV).

After receiving this information from the Lord, the children of Israel searched among themselves and found the culprit, a man named Achan, who says in verse 21, "When I saw among the spoils a beautiful Babylonian garment, two hundred shekels of silver, and a wedge of gold weighing fifty shekels, I coveted them and took them. And there they are, hidden in the earth in the midst of my tent, with the silver under it" (NKJV).

Disobedience prevented Achan and the children of Israel from achieving further victory over the wicked. Because of his actions, Achan became accursed through his theft and deception. The Lord couldn't give them further victory because of Achan's wicked deed. So when executing God's principle of claiming, remember to Worship, Praise, and Obey.

Summary

1. Types of Giving

Costless Giving - turn over the possession or control of some thing to someone without cost or exchange
Faith Promise Giving - identify the gift you want to receive and promise, before you receive it, to give it

2. Characteristics of a Gift

Given with a willing mind
Measurable
Life-giving to others and self
Given cheerfully
Given in accordance with what you have
May be given on the spur of the moment
Must be given unselfishly

3. Giving Cycle

Fertilize Ground.
Plant Seeds
Dig out Weeds.
Feed/Water.

Chapter 8
Provider Viewpoint: Saving

I remember when I was a teenager and I asked my grandfather if I could have a car. He agreed with one stipulation: I had to save for it. So I began to save diligently for my car, and after a short period of time I had enough money to purchase my first car. That experience taught me that anything worth having is worth the effort to save for it.

Today, the direct opposite is the case for most people. The focus of our present day society is on having it now, your way. We have been conditioned to believe everything and anything is accessible to us now. You name it, we are surrounded by instant everything: photographs, credit (cards), mail, food, etc. It's no surprise we don't feel the need to save: saving requires time and effort.

The invention and rapid expansion of credit cards grant us instant access to items we would have had to save for in the past. We have been conditioned to believe that the things we want are more important than saving the money it takes to acquire them. Our society's financial outlook has shifted from the amount of assets a person has (wealth) to the level of his creditworthiness, i.e., an individual's ability to make monthly payments (be a good debtor). So the value of saving is diminished. It is a lack of savings that contributes to financial lack or mediocrity. This lack of savings will at best leave you where you are. Savings will always take you higher than you've been before and cause you to accomplish more than ever before.

Let's take a look at "savers" from the Bible to illustrate this point. The Bible states in Genesis 39:4-5 that Joseph, while at Potiphar's house, was in charge of Potiphar's household. This included, of course, Potiphar's finances (Joseph was a financial consultant). So the Lord prospered everything Joseph managed in the household. After being taken before Pharaoh, Joseph displayed this same financial wisdom when he instructed Pharaoh to take (save) a fifth of the harvest during the seven years of abundance. It was that thought which took Joseph to the second-highest position in Egypt.

Another example: David desired to build God a house (2 Samuel 7:2-3). Although God said David's son Solomon would build the house (2 Samuel 7:12, 13), David prepared for the building of the temple by saving for it (2 Samuel 8:7-12). It was by David's saving that something great (temple), which had never been done before, was accomplished in Israel.

The situations of Joseph and David highlight two principles of saving:

1) Savings can help you to survive and thrive during lean times. The Bible says that the people brought Joseph all of their money, livestock, land, and eventually their freedom (Genesis 47:14, 16, 20, 25), and yet Joseph was able to provide food for the entire country and beyond, just from saving 20% of Egypt's income during the prosperous years.

2) Money allocated toward what you desire can help you to purchase/ build large dollar items without acquiring great debt.

There are many people who, because they can't afford to now, say once they "get rich" they will put money in the bank. They associate saving with being rich, when in reality, as we observed with Joseph and David, it's a higher thought. This higher thought grants power and the ability to make choices, to meet your goals, and to acquire wealth, something debtors believe they are unable to do. Possessing savings frees your mind from focusing exclusively on debt. For you reap what you sow. If you spend more, then you reap the result--you have less money. If you sow savings, then you reap the benefit--you have more money.

The most widely accepted amount to save is 10% of your gross (before deductions) or net (take home) pay. The level of savings is based on the individual. Generally, 1-3 months of your salary is good. Certainly, there are many who are in such dire straits that they can't afford to save the full 10%, and they may think they can't save. "The Pickle Jar" by A. W. Cobb in ***Chicken Soup for the Parent's Soul***, pp. 2-4, tells of putting coins aside at the end of each day and depositing them in a savings account at intentional intervals every week, or when the jar is full, or whatever works as one way to start saving. This savings technique is a good starting point, because trouble saving comes from setting your initial goals too high. The idea of saving is not necessarily to emphasize the amount, but to establish and maintain the habit and benefit from interest accumulating and compounding over time. The amount you're financially able to save may be nowhere near the amount you desire to save, but remember this: there are some tasks which require such time and effort that they can't be accomplished instantaneously. God created the world in six days (levels). He didn't lament that He hadn't yet created His ultimate goal--Man--during the initial five days. He did the work of the day with designs to reach His goal. So no matter what "day" you are on, do the work of that "day" before moving to the next (saving level).

Your funds should be placed in a savings vehicle which is liquid (easily accessible) and preserves your principal (possesses low risk). Such savings vehicles would include Passbook Savings, U.S. Savings Bonds, and Money Market Mutual Funds.

For a **Passbook Savings Account**, you take your money to a bank. The bank in turn agrees to hold your money and return a percentage of interest to you. Passbook Savings provide protection of an individual's principal (original investment) through what's called FDIC insurance. This insurance guarantees that your money will be available whenever you want it, without concern for loss. It comes at a price, though. Interest rates on savings accounts are extremely low, currently ranging from 1-3%. The rates are so low because you are paying for this insurance and receive low interest paid on your deposit.

U.S. Savings Bonds are products of the U.S. Government. These are loans you make to "Uncle Sam" guaranteed by the "full faith and credit of the United States Government". This means that Savings Bonds are backed by Uncle Sam's ability to tax us, his "nieces and nephews," and print money. The interest paid on these bonds is usually higher than is paid for passbook savings, and the bonds can be purchased from and are redeemable after you hold them for six months without a fee at any banking institution. U.S. Savings Bonds also provide tax advantages in that there are no state and local taxes. There is also no federal income tax on earning until you redeem the bonds, if you so choose (see your tax advisor for more details). Interest on savings bonds is tax-free if used for education (with restrictions).

A **Money Market Mutual Fund** is simply a portfolio of short-term money market securities. These securities consist of Treasury Bills, commercial paper, etc. They are designed to be extremely safe and conservative. Money Market Mutual Funds can be found at most major fund families, brokers, and banks.

Of the three liquid savings vehicles, money markets offer the greatest flexibility and benefits for your savings. They are low risk, pay a greater return than a passbook savings account, offer check writing, are available in tax-free versions, etc. Generally, Money Market Mutual Funds require a minimum of $250-$1000 opening balance along with a minimum monthly savings deposit.

Positive Reasons for Saving

Savings are so important that even God kept a remnant of 7000 worshippers during a time of great idolatry by the entire country of Israel (1 Kings 19:18). God's people were very dear to Him. For Him to make efforts on His part to keep a remnant proves three positive things about savings:

1) "Food during lean times". Savings keep something valuable from being wiped out in times of adversity.
2) Seeds for replenishment. Savings provide a means (seed) to replenish, restore, and exceed former levels.
3) Something greater than present self. Another reason to save is for the generation to come, so they can see the blessing God gave when He brought you out of poverty.

Food During Lean Times There may be times when a farmer won't reap a harvest from his sowing, for whatever reason. Possessing savings ensures that he still has income during lean times, because others didn't save any food and will pay higher prices for what the farmer has stored. That's what Joseph did in Egypt. He took a portion of his prosperity and saved it during the economic boom. As a result of this, he prospered even more during lean times.

Today a family may encounter a crisis that affects them economically. For example, a spouse may become disabled or die. An event like this can be catastrophic to a family's finances. To lessen the impact of such a catastrophe, I suggest a form of savings called insurance. Insurance is a form of savings by which a family is protected from financial loss due to catastrophic events like disability and death. In our quest to prosper financially, we tend to overlook the role insurance plays in our personal finances.

Let's say that you are following your financial plan perfectly when you or your spouse unexpectedly becomes disabled or dies. Suddenly, a source of income you were depending on is gone. Such a loss of income can throw the best-laid plans into chaos. Even if you are fortunate enough to have saved for "lean times," your savings is a short-term solution at best. During such unexpected crises, any savings, retirement fund, and investments you may have accumulated are at risk of being consumed to maintain your standard of living. Insurance protects these resources during a crisis event.

My insurance agent once told me a story comparing insurance to an umbrella that protects your financial lifestyle (savings, home, car, investments, etc.) from the unexpected storms of life (death, hospitalization, and disability, etc.). As an "umbrella," insurance provides a measure of protection as you weather those "storms of life". My "storm of life" came when my wife was unexpectedly diagnosed with a condition which left her temporarily disabled. After exhausting her paid sick leave, her condition still called for her to take an unpaid, indefinite leave of absence from her job. All at once my wife's salary was removed from our budget. We possessed savings, investments, and retirement funds, which we could tap into if needed, but tapping those resources would disrupt our financial plan. Fortunately, when we married I had the foresight to purchase income and mortgage disability insurance policies. With those policies in force, I knew that our financial plan wouldn't suffer from her unpaid leave of absence. After we met certain criteria, the income disability policy would provide a pre-arranged, tax-free level of income for a period of one year, while the mortgage disability policy would pay our mortgage for up to three years. These policies made a potential financial catastrophe into a financially manageable event.

Seeds for Replenishment Ask any successful farmer about the importance of timing, and he will tell you that timing can mean the difference between prospering and starving. When a farmer initially plants his seed, he doesn't plant all of his seed at once. He holds some seed back because he realizes that replenishment is a key to maintaining a constant flow of fruit (i.e., when his original planting is ready for harvest, he has additional seed for sowing).

Something Greater than Present Self Whether saving for a house, college, investment, or something else, saving in this manner challenges you to grow. It literally pulls you to the next level. Many people say they want to go to the next financial level but continue to respond using the thoughts of the current and previous levels, i.e., spending everything they get their hands on and buying consumables on credit. This type of thought comes with a price, and that price is interest. Instead, save for what you want and let your ascension to the next level in your finances pull you to what you want.

Negative Reason for Saving

It has been established that the condition of your heart can have a direct bearing on your giving. The same can be said for saving as well. It's the condition of your heart that can distort how you view money, leading to potentially dangerous consequences. Stinginess and greed can cause improper viewing of saving.

Greed is wanting or taking all that one can get, with no thought for others' needs; desiring more than one needs. As I indicated earlier, greed is a condition of the heart and causes a host of problems to your finances. The very nature of greed distorts your view of money and severely limits its flow. For money to multiply as well as bless you, it must be able to flow freely from you to others and from others to you. And as the parable of the Rich Fool states (Luke 12:16-21), greed can kill you! Greed leads to very serious health problems, which tends to lead to worry, which can ultimately lead to death.

Stinginess is defined as sharing or spending grudgingly or only through necessity. People suffering from stinginess view savings through the filter of scarcity, believing that their savings can't be replenished or increased by their actions and that conservation, and not giving of their resources, is a key component to prospering. Second Corinthians 9:6-8 (NKJV) expounds on this condition of the heart as Paul provides insight into how your money can be affected by the condition of your heart.

v6 But this I say: He who sows sparingly will also reap sparingly, and he who sows bountifully will also reap bountifully.
v7 So let each one give as he purposes in his heart, not grudgingly or of necessity; for God loves a cheerful giver.
v8 And God is able to make all grace abound toward you, that you, always having all sufficiency in all things, may have an abundance for every good work.

I believe that Paul was sharing with the Corinthian church the secrets for financial prosperity. The amount you give and the condition of your heart must be in alignment to properly reap. In other words, if you felt obligated to give a bountiful sum of money and your "heart wasn't in it," then that gift was counter-productive. Because your heart and gift didn't agree, God did not make all grace abound toward you that you might acquire abundance. A story of reluctant giving with no acquisition of abundance is in Acts 5:1-10. Conversely, if you sowed a small gift, and your heart was in it, even though you may have sown a small amount of money, because your giving and heart were in alignment, you were able to reap a return. Both Mark (12:42-44) and Luke (21:2-4) describe Jesus praising the woman who gave her all, though it was a tiny sum. Second Corinthians 8:12 teaches, "For if there is first a willing mind, it is accepted according to what one has, and not according to what he does not have" (NKJV).

As the parable of talents indicates (Matthew 25:14-28), if you are not increasing, then you can't help but decrease, because we don't live in a static environment where things remain the same. Savings, no matter how small or large, are the seeds of control. Savings will enable you to prosper even during lean or adverse times. You now control a portion of your finances that debt once controlled. Remember, save for positive reasons and you will see positive results. The blessing in the end is greater than in the beginning.

Summary

Source of financial problems. Some from incorrect spending. Majority from incorrect sowing.

Results of planting correctly. Seed to plant again. Seed to eat (use on whatever we want).

Results of poor planting methods. Only short-term pleasure from seeds scattered on the path. Lack of seeds to plant again from seed (money) choked (taken away) by thorns.

Principles for accumulating the great wealth God has laid up for the just. Assets attract money. Liabilities repel money.

The way you obey those principles will determine your level of financial success.
Matthew 25:21 NKJV says, "His lord said to him, 'Well done, good and faithful servant; you were faithful over a few things, I will make you ruler over many things. Enter into the joy of your lord.'"

Chapter 9
Increase

Increase is a mindset. Therefore, your mind needs to be conditioned for increase. Society's interest in the material conditions us for accumulating debt, not generating increase. In the previous chapters, we discussed four financial viewpoints of management (spending, saving, debt, and giving). Equally important are the four financial viewpoints of increase (work, giving, savings, investment). Although each financial viewpoint of increase is different, each one is characterized by (provides) one of the same traits: growth, income, and/or asset preservation. Four principles for developing a mindset for increase are: Diligence, Generosity, Allocation, and Diversification.

Diligence is defined as work done with careful, steady effort. Diligence allows you to see your success on a daily basis. As a whole, people have diverted their focus away from this principle to embrace the desire for quick wealth. The trappings of success, not the principles that brought it about, are glorified. This is an example of the cart before the horse syndrome, and without help there is no sign of turning back. That's why people are searching for the latest gimmick to generate wealth. Gimmicks don't generate wealth, but following the correct principles does. Proverbs 10:4 NIV states, "Lazy hands make a man poor, but diligent hands bring wealth." Diligence allows you to plan out your success with careful and steady effort. Diligence begins with a plan for your success and ends with goals reached by persistent and consistent effort.

Generosity is a willingness to give or share unselfishly. Generosity is the foundation for the mindset of increase. Proverbs 11:25 states that a generous man will prosper; he who refreshes others will himself be refreshed. People tend to view increase incorrectly as flowing in only one direction: to them. In fact, increase flows in both directions, to you from

from others and from others to you. As people digress from generosity, stinginess develops. Proverbs 28:22 NIV states, "A stingy man is eager to get rich and is unaware that poverty awaits him." Reverse this thought process by learning how to be content with what you have. Generosity is a natural progression from contentment with what you have.

Allocation, or setting things apart for a specific purpose, and distributing those things in shares or according to a plan is the key to prospering. Allocation of your resources such as (money, time, and/or effort), will yield either a blended or an overall return. This is so because each financial category performs differently at any given time. One category may be just starting to grow while you are reaping in another. For example, let's say that you have just given $1,000.00 to a charity, and based on what we have learned (or are learning), if the cycle of giving is followed correctly, you'll reap an increase. Although this is true, there are a number of instances where we don't reap the next day. The process takes time. If we don't have monies allocated in other categories of increase, it will seem as if, although we are using our money in a category of increase, we are going backward financially. Now, let's travel a month in the future. You need funds right away but don't have a surplus. Then resentment grows and you become depressed, thinking giving doesn't yield an increase, because you put all of your "eggs" in one basket and failed to take advantage of the other three categories of increase while your gift was growing. Allocation is designed to assist you in picking the right mix that yields the greatest return with the least risk possible.

King Solomon, the world's wealthiest businessman, spoke of this increase principle when he stated in Ecclesiastes 11:5-6 NIV:

v5 As you do not know the path of the wind, or how the body is formed in a mother's womb, so you cannot understand the work of God, the Maker of all things.
v6 Sow your seed in the morning, and at evening let not your hands be idle, for you do not know which will succeed, whether this or that, or whether [or when] both will do equally well.

Diversification is spreading your money across investment opportunities within a certain investment type to achieve the delicate balance between risk and return. This principle of investing helps reduce risk and maximize return.

For example, let's say you are an investor who is looking for low-risk investments. Low-risk investments primarily include:

a) Savings Accounts
b) Money Market Accounts
c) CDs
d) Savings Bonds
e) T-Bills, Notes, etc.

Using diversification, you are able to reduce the risk of losing principal as well as position yourself for a return even if some of the investments don't produce the expected yield. The table below examines the use of CDs, Saving Bonds, and diversification. If we were fortunate enough to lock in a $1000.00 CD Rate of 8% for five years, that would be great. But, if interest rates skyrocketed to 14% three years later (after your initial purchase), you would lose an excellent opportunity for a higher return. Fortunately, you didn't "put all of your eggs in one basket". Instead, you also invested in Savings Bonds, which in this scenario are returning a current market rate of 12%. Because of diversification you're able to reap the highest yields from both investments instead of taking a chance in receiving a lower return had you chosen just one.

Interest Rate

	CD	Bonds	Diversify
Year One	8.00%	5.00%	6.50%
Year Two	8.00%	5.00%	6.50%
Year Three	8.00%	12.00%	10.00%
Year Four	8.00%	12.00%	10.00%
Year Five	8.00%	12.00%	10.00%
Total	8.00%	9.20%	8.60%

Earnings

	CD	Bonds	Diversify
Year One	$80.00	$ 50.00	$ 65.00
Year Two	$80.00	$ 50.00	$ 65.00
Year Three	$80.00	$120.00	$100.00
Year Four	$80.00	$120.00	$100.00
Year Five	$80.00	$120.00	$100.00
Total	$400.00	$460.00	$430.00

By looking at the investment table above you can easily see that had you invested all of your money in the bonds you would have realized the highest return. But it's easier to invest in hindsight. In year one, there was no indication that market interest rates were going to increase. By the same token, the market could have taken a downturn resulting in the following:

Interest Rate

	CD	Bonds	Diversify
Year One	8.00%	5.00%	6.50%
Year Two	8.00%	5.00%	6.50%
Year Three	8.00%	3.00%	6.00%
Year Four	8.00%	3.00%	5.50%
Year Five	8.00%	3.00%	6.00%
Total	8.00%	3.80%	6.00%

Earnings

	CD	Bonds	Diversify
Year One	$80.00	$50.00	$65.00
Year Two	$80.00	$50.00	$65.00
Year Three	$80.00	$30.00	$60.00
Year Four	$80.00	$30.00	$55.00
Year Five	$80.00	$30.00	$55.00
Total	$400.00	$190.00	$300.00

Diversification allows for a higher return with much less risk. Your investment risk is spread across several investments, decreasing the likelihood of loss of your entire principal in a downturn of a single investment. In this case, the fixed CD rate cushioned the loss from the drop in bonds.

Matthew 25:21 NKJV says, "His lord said to him, 'Well done, good and faithful servant; you were faithful over a few things, I will make you ruler over many things. Enter into the joy of your lord." God is pleased when we trust God and use wisely the gifts God bestows, and blessings follow.

Summary

Four categories of Increase

Working
Giving
Saving
Investing

Four Principles of Increase

Diligence
Generosity
Allocation
Diversification

Reduce risk and maximize return by putting money in several vehicles and several types of investments.

Chapter 10 Producer Viewpoint: Investment

Once you enter the realm of provider, God wants you to dwell there. To enable you to remain a provider (as He is), God made a way for you to use a portion of money from the provisional realm as a means of increase. By taking some of your earnings generated by your role as provider, you can now produce or increase.

The first producer category I will discuss in depth is investing. When inflation and interest rates are low, and the economic cycle is in a state of recession or recovery, savvy investors are looking to invest. Stocks and Mutual Funds should not be viewed as "get rich quick" schemes. They should be viewed as they are, high-end investments, usually yielding the highest returns, but also possessing the highest risk. While high returns are most desirable when investing, it is also important to base investments on your personal investment goals.

Goals of Investing

Your personal goals strongly influence how you choose to invest your money. I have identified four common financial goals:

1) Having adequate funds for retirement
2) Additional growth asset purchases
3) Additional income
4) An inheritance for heirs.

To better help you determine and focus on your personal investment goals, I've included an overview of the four types of goals listed above.

Retirement Retirement Investing is the investment of financial surplus during prime working years to ensure financial survival during a time when our ability to work and earn has declined. As we age and our physical bodies decline, our ability to work and earn money declines as well. The wise person prepares for this inevitability by investing financial surplus during prime working years to ensure continued financial survival during retirement. Investing for retirement first allows you to benefit from compounding returns, usually in a tax-deferred or tax-free status. Compounding occurs when interest earned is added to principal, earning additional interest in future years.

When you choose an investment, a Certificate of Deposit (CD) for example, remember that the frequency of compounding can have an effect on your return. Annual compounding is common, but in my experience, some banks and credit unions offer semi-annual or even monthly compounding if their customers invest larger sums of money and/or agree to a longer CD term. If you have two competing banks offering the same CD interest rate and minimum deposit, if Bank A is offering a monthly compounded rate and Bank B is offering an annual compounded rate, selecting monthly compounding is the better choice. Let's say that you have inherited $10,000 and you open a CD. Take a look at the return on your money after one year:

Situation A
$10,000
6% Rate Compounded Monthly
One Year: $10,616.78

Situation B
$10,000
6% Rate Compounded Annually
One Year: $10,600.00

As you can see, the monthly compounding provides a better yield, because the earned interest is added to the principal, resulting in a new principal balance monthly. Interest is calculated using the new higher principal balance.

Vehicles of Investing for Retirement The primary vehicles used for retirement investing are

a) 401(k) plans for employees of for-profit companies
b) 403(b) plans for employees of non-profit organizations (such as churches)
c) IRAs
d) Roth IRAs
e) Annuities.

Self-employed people and business owners can set up similar retirement plans (see your financial advisor for details).

401(k) Plans The 401(k) plans are company-based retirement plans. They are by far one of the best retirement vehicles available if you are a regular wage earner (receive a W-2 from your employer in a for-profit company). As a result of the Growth and Tax Relief Reconciliation Act of 2001 (TRA 2001), employees are allowed to make salary reduction contributions in accordance with the following table.

Year	Maximum Contribution
2002	$11,000
2003	$12,000
2004	$13,000
2005	$14,000
2006	$15,000
2007	Indexed

An added bonus is the election by some employers' plans to provide direct employer contributions. These contributions are based on a percentage of your salary. Employee contributions are made from gross income. These contributions are also free from federal withholding tax. Having these contributions taken from your gross income reduces your overall tax bill. The contribution, although free from state income tax, is still subject to Social Security and Medicare taxes. Pre-retirement withdrawals are subject to taxation and an additional 10% early withdrawal penalty. Any increase in the value of your plan is tax-deferred, meaning you don't pay taxes on the money you contribute until the original contribution and/or gains are withdrawn from your account.

403(b) Plans The 403(b) plans are tax-exempt company retirement plans. They are extremely similar to 401(k) plans with only minor variances, such as the fact that 403(b) plans are not permitted to invest in individual stocks and bonds, and plan participants over the age of 50 are allowed to contribute additional catch-up amounts.

IRAs. IRAs (Individual Retirement Accounts) allow individuals who may or may not have exceeded their contribution limit on their 401(k) or 403(b) accounts to make individual contributions to their retirement funds. An IRA is similar to 401(k) and 403(b) in that the contributions can grow tax-deferred and in some cases are tax-deductible. Another similarity IRAs share with 403(b) is the eligibility of participants to make catch-up contributions. Unlike the 401(k) and 403(b) accounts, there is a much lower maximum contribution limit (see table below), along with income restrictions which could limit or eliminate the tax deductibility of your IRA. Ask your financial or tax advisor for specific details.

Year	Maximum Contribution	Maximum Contribution Age 50 or Older
2002	$3,000	$3,500
2003	$3,000	$3,500
2004	$3,000	$3,500
2005	$4,000	$4,500
2006	$4,000	$5,000
2008	$5,000	$6,000
2009	Indexed	Base Indexed contribution (plus $1000)

Roth IRAs A Roth IRA offers you the capability of making non-deductible after-tax contributions to your account. If you maintain the account for a minimum of five years and you are at least 59-1/2 years old, the withdrawals are not includible in your gross income for tax purposes. If you meet all the qualifications, then you don't have to pay income tax at all on these types of accounts. There are other benefits as well, such as the ability to withdraw the money from your account after five years tax-free, if the money is used to purchase your first home (lifetime cap of $10,000). Unlike a regular IRA, a Roth IRA doesn't require distribution after age 70-1/2. Limits for contributions to a Roth IRA are the same as those for an IRA, listed in the table above.

Annuities Annuities allow your money to grow tax-deferred just like 401(k) plans, 403(b) plans, and IRAs. Early withdrawals are penalized if taken before the age of 59-1/2.

Annuities are similar to a Roth in that they don't provide any deductible contributions. There are two major benefits that make annuities attractive to some people. First, unlike the other retirement vehicles, there is no annual contribution limit. Second, there are no mandatory age withdrawals, so you can leave your money in an annuity for as long as you like. The annuitant may choose the installment refund annuity settlement option. If the annuitant dies before receiving total income payments equal to the purchase price of the annuity, the payments continue to the beneficiary until they equal the purchase price.

There are two types of annuities, fixed and variable. A fixed annuity is one in which the sponsor agrees to pay a fixed rate of return on your money. A variable annuity is one in which your money is invested by the sponsor in a portfolio that may consist of stocks, mutual funds, etc. You may want to consider an annuity only after you've exhausted all of your other retirement vehicles, because the maintenance fees on annuities are normally higher than for the other investment vehicles, and it would require several years of compounding returns to outweigh the impact of the higher maintenance fees.

Choosing Your Retirement Vehicle Understanding the available retirement vehicles can be challenging in and of itself, but choosing can be even more difficult.

To simplify your choice, for most wage-earning individuals, your contributions' freedom from federal withholding makes it advantageous for you to contribute to your company-based plan first, such as a 401(k) or 403(b). These plans offer higher contribution amounts, tax-deferment, and current income tax savings. In the case of a 401(k), your employer matches up to a certain percentage of your contributions.

After you have contributed the maximum allowable to your 401(k) or 403(b), the next tier of investment choices is Deductible IRAs. These plans offer similar benefits, with these restrictions: smaller contribution amounts, no employer match, and income restrictions.

Of the remaining investment choices, your income level and your present amount of money available for savings would influence your decision. However, in most cases the next tier investment vehicle would be a Roth IRA. The Roth IRA lacks the benefit of a present tax deduction but replaces that with tax-free withdrawals. There may be certain individuals for whom income level, amount available for savings, and preferred timing of taxation will be different, and a non-deductible IRA would be more beneficial. The choice is based on other factors best addressed individually. In most cases, however, if both of these investments don't offer the present tax deduction, but one is tax-deferred and the other is tax-free, the latter is a better investment choice.

Rounding out the list would be an annuity. Consider contributing to an annuity last. Due to the insurance component, annuities carry higher fees compared to other retirement vehicles, and contributions to annuities are not tax-deductible. Some people who have a significant amount of money, who also have a period of time available to allow for the compounding of the investment to outweigh the fees, and whose financial plans call for more money toward retirement than is allowed by the other retirement vehicles, would benefit the most from purchasing an annuity.

Asset/Growth To properly increase your net worth, you need to manage what you earn now and invest for growth. Investing for growth is the next investment allocation in financial prosperity. This type of investing requires patience, because in most cases it takes time for the value of these types of investments to increase. The goal is the acquisition of assets that have the potential and/or history to increase in value.

Vehicles for Asset Growth Investing in asset/growth vehicles enables you to invest tax-deferred, in that you don't incur tax liabilities until you sell at a gain, and you are allowed under current tax rules to offset your gains against your losses for tax purposes.

The primary vehicles used for asset/growth investing are Series EE/I Savings Bonds, stocks, Index or tax-sensitive growth mutual funds, precious metals, and undeveloped real estate.

Savings Bonds Series EE/I Savings Bonds are instruments of debt. You are lending money to the United States Government, and they will in turn pay you the original investment along with interest. Both types of bonds can be purchased directly from the Department of the Treasury or your local bank. The Series EE bonds are purchased for 1/2 their face value. (If you want to purchase a $50 Series EE Bond, it will cost $25.) The interest this bond pays to you is 90% of the average of five-year Treasury yields, which is published by the Department of the Treasury every May and November. Series EE Bonds purchased on and after May 1, 2005 will earn fixed rates of interest set at time of issue.

The I-Bonds are purchased at face value. (If you want to purchase a $100 I-Bond, it will cost $100.) The interest this bond pays you is based on two components: the fixed rate and the semi-annual inflation rate. The fixed rate is issued to the bond at purchase and will not change over the life of the bond. For example, if you went out and purchased an I-bond today and the fixed rate was 4%, then that rate would not change over the life of the bond. The semi-annual inflation rate portion is tied to the inflation rate. This rate is determined by the Consumer Price Index-Urban Consumers (CPI-U), which is also published every May and November. This portion of the I-Bonds interest rate does change based on the CPI-U to enable you to continue earning interest above the rate of inflation.

The interest on both types of bonds increases the value of the bond monthly and compounds semi-annually. Although interest is generated monthly and bonds are instruments of debt, not ownership, this investment vehicle is listed as a growth-type asset, because the increase in value of the investment is allowed to grow tax-deferred (if you choose) until it is redeemed. This enables you to keep your investment and increase your wealth without having to pay taxes on the increase in wealth as it occurs. Taxes that must be paid from current income affect your current standard of living. For example, a mutual fund's capital gains are taxable in the year generated. This presents a dilemma: if you don't want to sell the fund, you must pay income taxes out of your current income.

Stocks Stocks are similar to savings bonds in that they are allowed to experience growth in their value tax-deferred until they are sold, and they enable you to benefit from compounding returns. The similarities end there, however. Stocks are instruments (or shares) of ownership in companies, while savings bonds are debt instruments of the U.S. Government. The value of these shares can change based on several factors, such as profit gain, profit loss, economic climate, and emotions.

Economic climate and emotion are the main culprits influencing short-term stock prices. The current peaks and valleys in the market are based on both the economic climate and emotion. Those and other factors would probably be best discussed at length in a book dedicated to stocks.

Stock investing is a difficult but learnable skill. I have identified three important skills for successful stock investing: evaluation, selection, and management (how and when to buy or sell). Each of these skills requires a certain level of competence to maximize stock earnings. The majority of stock investment books teach how to evaluate and select stocks that are undervalued and are poised to increase in value. But what of the stocks that are over-valued or expected to decrease? By limiting yourself to undervalued stocks that you expect to increase in a booming market, you are missing out on potentially large profits through solid management during a downturn.

Stock managers, by utilizing solid management techniques such as short-selling, their years of training, and their financial savvy, have greater odds of generating a profit for their clients during a downturn than most individuals managing their own stocks just on the basis of what they learned from a book. Each transaction is an emotional event for the novice investor. On the other hand, a trained professional stock manager is not emotionally attached to a stock; his objective is to earn an overall profit for his client. An experienced stock professional knows how to minimize losses and maximize gains. Most novice investors don't possess this skill.

Case in point: several years ago, when stocks were booming, I received a "tip" from a relative to buy a stock. Now, let me caution you, although I know infinitely more about stocks now, at that time I knew very little about them. Immediately after I purchased the stock, its value increased about 10%. I was ecstatic and wanted to see more. Alas, that would not be: over the course of two months that stock took me on an emotional roller coaster ride because I had a significant (at that time) amount of money involved. Eventually I arrived at a point that I couldn't take it any-more, and after losing 40% of my original investment value, I sold at a loss. Over the next six months the stock split and increased in value. So what's my point? Had I been well versed in stock management (when to buy and sell), perhaps I could have avoided the emotional roller coaster ride and sold after the original 10% gain or utilized other management techniques such as short-selling to profit in the downturn.

It bears mentioning again that stock investing can be quite challenging to a novice. As challenging as stock investment is, I'm aware that some of you may possess the competence to invest in stocks on your own. Still, I take the position of the master in Matthew 25. He delivered his goods (money) into the hands of his servants. The possession of money didn't make the master an investment expert. Wise investment calls for the preservation of capital, and the master realized that someone he trusted whose duty was to increase his investment would better serve his capital. Therefore, I would advise that you seek additional guidance before attempting to purchase stock.

Mutual Funds Index (or Tax-sensitive) Growth Mutual Funds are examples of pools of money invested in a fund of stocks whose purpose is to maximize growth while minimizing tax liability, two characteristics needed for maximum asset growth.

Precious Metals Precious Metals, like gold or silver, are also growth-type investments. They are not taxed until a capital gain is realized, and unlike other growth investments (besides I-bonds and real estate), they provide a hedge against inflation. (If inflation increases, the value of the precious metal normally increases along with inflation.) As long-term investments, however, precious metals don't compare favorably to stock and real estate.

Undeveloped Real Estate Undeveloped Real Estate can also be a tremendous growth asset. This growth asset is rather unique in comparison to other growth assets in that, although your taxes are paid annually in the form of real estate taxes, unlike the tax on other investments, real estate taxes are deductible on your personal income tax form, provided you itemize. One potential drawback in purchasing undeveloped land is that it can "tie up" or consume cash and take years to yield an increase.

There are circumstances where this buy-and-hold strategy is successful. I remember growing up in my small hometown. When I was about eight years old, my grandfather and I would sometimes travel to the little country store. It was very small, no larger than the average tool shed. The caretaker of the store died about ten years later, and the property remained vacant for several years afterward. However, if you drive by that property today, you see there a brand new McDonald's restaurant!!!

Who would have known that the small store sat on property which would one day be home to a McDonald's restaurant? The property values surrounding the restaurant immediately increased.

So what am I saying? I'm saying that if you have some patience, knowledge, and available cash for real estate taxes and other expenses, you could possibly benefit from purchasing a piece of land which could someday be home to a company or a retailer.

Choosing Your Growth Vehicles Taxes on increases from savings bonds, stocks, and precious metals can be deferred. Taxes on undeveloped real estate are payable annually but deductible for those who itemize. Taxes on increases from mutual funds are payable annually. Tax liability may help decide the preferable Growth Vehicle.

Income OK, let's review. You've invested money for retirement and for growth assets. Ten years into the future, those growth assets have appreciated considerably, and you would like to supplement your income. Then you must consider investing your monies in an income-producing asset. The goal of owning an income-producing asset is to derive income (cash flow) from an asset over the life of the asset. As people grow older and retirement looms ahead, "risk aversion" develops. As a result of this condition, investors are not as concerned with increasing the value of their investments, but they are definitely interested in preserving the capital (the existing value of the investments) and reaping income.

Investment Vehicles Several examples of such investments are bonds, CDs, mutual funds, dividend-producing stocks, and real estate investment trusts.

<u>Bonds</u> Bonds are instruments of debt. Whenever an individual purchases a bond, the individual lends money to the corporate, municipal, or federal entity. Although each bond is different, bonds still share three common characteristics: face value, maturity date, and interest. Face value means the amount of money you lend to the entity. Maturity date is the date the entity promises to pay you back. Interest is the income payable to you, usually on a semi-annual basis.

Here's an example of a bond transaction: instead of stock, XYZ Company decides to issue corporate bonds. They issue the following bond: $10,000, 30-year bond, at 7 percent interest. The semi-annual interest you would earn as income would be $10,000 x 7% = $350.00.

Before purchasing any type of bond, an investor needs to check the creditworthiness of the bond issuer. This is done to limit the likelihood of bond issuer default (your not receiving your money back!!). To assist the investor there are two major credit rating services, Standard & Poor's and Moody's Investor Service. These services objectively rate the creditworthiness of, and assign a rating to, the bond issuer.

The top four ratings of these services are given to what are called investment grade bonds. These are the top four ratings in decreasing credit rating:

Moody's Aaa, Aa, A, Baa
Standard & Poor's AAA, AA, A, BBB
Any ratings lower than the ones listed above would be considered non-investment grade bonds. Non-investment grade bonds normally pay more interest, but do so because of the assumption of greater risk. Listed below are three of the better-known types of bonds:

1) Corporate Bonds are bonds issued by corporations. They are taxable at the federal, state,and local levels.
2) Municipal Bonds are bonds issued by municipalities. They are federally non-taxable and non-taxable to residents of the issuing state.
3) Treasury Bonds are bonds issued by the Department of the Treasury. Interest on Treasury Bonds is federally taxable but state tax-free.

Individual bonds are available for purchase through a discount broker.

Certificates of Deposit (CDs) A CD consists of money you lend to your bank. These instruments are similar to bonds in that they pay interest. A CD differs from a bond in that there is an early withdrawal penalty if money is removed from a CD prior to maturity. A CD doesn't experience fluctuations in value and is insured by FDIC Insurance, which comes at a cost. The interest paid on a CD is almost always lower than that paid on a bond and is fully taxable at the federal and state levels.

Bond/Stock Mutual Funds Bond/Stock Mutual Funds are pools of money invested in the bond/stock market. Participating in a bond/stock fund enables the investor to benefit from diversification. Unlike individual bond/stock investing, bond/stock mutual fund investing spreads the risk among several bonds/securities in different industries and sectors. There are several other benefits to investors, such as professional fund management and accessibility to bonds/stocks they might not be able to afford to purchase alone (outside of a bond/stock fund).

Before you invest in a mutual fund, there are a few items you should evaluate. First, an investor must search for the lowest management fee. Participation in a bond/stock fund requires a management fee. This fee varies from fund to fund. The higher the fee, the more your overall return is reduced. Second, novice investors should avoid funds with sales loads. A sales load is a commission paid to a broker who sells mutual funds. A sales load mutual fund does not guarantee a greater return on investment than does a no-load (no sales charge) fund. Third, try to minimize operating expenses. Remember, if you minimize expenses you can increase profit margin, and operating expenses should not exceed 1.5%. Any fund which has expenses greater than 1.5% should be examined with caution. By law, gains from a mutual fund must be disbursed annually and are fully taxable in the year of distribution.

Stock Dividends Investors in individual stocks can earn income through dividends. Dividends are payments made to investors from the company's profits. Instead of reinvesting the money in the company, the officers of the company decide to share a percentage of the profit with investors through dividends. Corporations with a history of paying out dividends usually continue to do so as long as they remain profitable.

Dividends are normally paid out annually and are fully taxable in the year of distribution.

Real Estate Investment Trusts (REITs) Investors who want to invest in real estate, but don't want the potential headaches that being a property manager can bring, need not look any further: a REIT is appropriate.

A share in a REIT is stock in companies which invest in real estate. Dividends paid from REITs are fully taxable. One benefit to investing in REITs is the fact that you can purchase them very easily without a broker (or broker's fees) REIT's offer and possess good liquidity. These stocks are listed in the securities section of your local newspaper. These investments should be evaluated like regular stock. For those who are clueless about evaluating an individual REIT, a REIT mutual fund might be preferable.

Choosing an Income Vehicle Certificates of Deposit offer dependable income that is fully taxable. Gains from mutual funds are distributed annually and are fully taxable. Stock dividends are normally payable annually, and they are fully taxable in the year of distribution. Dividends from REITs and earnings on corporate bonds are fully taxable. Municipal bonds are exempt from federal income tax, so municipal and treasury bonds carry less tax liability than other income vehicles.

Ease of evaluation and purchase, liquidity, and dependability of income are other factors that may influence the preferences of the investor.

Inheritance "A good man leaves an inheritance to his children's children, But the wealth of the sinner is stored up for the righteous" (Proverbs 13:22, NKJV). An inheritance is money, property, or other valuables received by a descendant upon death of the bestower. The importance of an inheritance to a man's children is stated in chapter 13 of Proverbs. The author of Proverbs declares that a good man leaves such a large inheritance that it reaches his children's children.

Acquiring an inheritance helps your heirs start at a higher place economically than you did. Think how beneficial it would have been starting your adult lives with a financial boost from your grandparents or great-grandparents. Inheritance creates a family legacy. Take a look at famous and wealthy families. The Kennedys, for example, add new wealth each new generation. This wealth is added to the wealth from the previous generations. This is the final stage in investing. By choosing to focus on inheritance last, the parent enables the child to fully benefit from potential inheritance on the children while the children are young, in part because the parents are unable to fathom the benefit and value of leaving a true inheritance. Spending massive amounts of money buying your children the latest fads in clothes and games offers nothing in comparison to the benefit they would receive from your financial legacy. I'm not saying buying your children things is bad, but don't get caught up in debt doing so, spending all you have on things that will not outlast the credit card bills generated to pay for them. Teaching your children the value of money and ways to live frugally is much more beneficial to them than using your money to try to give them everything you didn't have growing up.

Levels of Investing

After determining your goal, the next step is to decide which level of investing you'll use to get you to your destination. Many other financial publications define these levels in degrees of risk. Although risk is a factor in investing, I feel that defining investments in terms of risk makes investing seem more frightening than it actually is. I believe that investments should be defined by the return and the way the return is determined. Because of this I have narrowed investments to three basic levels. They are:

1) Others.
2) Markets.
3) Self.

Others This type of investing is one in which the person or entity to whom you are lending money determines your return. Examples of "others" investments are CDs, Money Market Accounts, Savings Bonds, Treasury Notes & Bills, Cash Value Insurance policies, etc.

Markets This type of investing is one in which the market or other conditions determine your rate of return. The market is such a powerful indicator of return that it even indirectly affects the other types of investing. Examples of these types of investments are Stocks, Series EE/I Bonds, Variable Annuities, Primary Residence, Long-term Government Bonds,

Corporate Bonds, IRA, 401(k), (403(b), precious metals, commodities, etc.

Self This type of investing is one in which you determine the interest rate and/or potential return. "Self" investments are banks' favorites because the bank (for the most part) establishes the interest rate. Examples are any type of consumer loan, including credit cards; personal loans, mortgage loans, car loans, boat loans, and education loans. Buying investment real estate, and establishing a business, are additional ways you determine the rate of return based on your actions. The higher up you travel on the investment ladder, the more knowledge and capital are required. At the Self level, conventional wisdom recommends that when you issue a loan to someone you tie the loan with security, credit history, or someone else's guaranteeing the loan (surety) for the debtor. The Bible warns people against serving as surety for others (Proverbs 6:1-5, 11:15, 17:18, 20:16, 22:26, and 27:13). I would suggest that if a potential borrower cannot offer security or credit history, but has someone willing to guarantee the loan, you suggest that the one willing to guarantee the loan become the lender.

The Bible, in Deuteronomy 28:12 (NKJV), confirms that this Self form is the highest form of investing. In this verse the Lord is bestowing his richest blessing on the Children of Israel. It reads: "The LORD will open to you His good treasure, the heavens, to give the rain to your land in its season, and to bless all the work of your hand." The final sentence in this verse indicates the result of having the blessing rest on your finances: "You shall lend to many nations, but you shall not borrow." When you have the power to determine when and how much an individual pays you back, you've reached the highest level of investing.

Ability vs. Risk in Investing

Now that your goals have been determined and you've decided what level of investing to use, the next step is to analyze your ability to invest and the risk involved. Simply stated, ability means skill, expertness, or talent; and risk means the chance of injury or loss. It's my belief that, contrary to current popular opinion, investments should be made based on your own or your investor's ability. The investment climate appears to focus on risk first and foremost. Certainly, risk is important and something which should be reviewed and observed with wisdom, but I believe that God's Word states in the following passage the way we should invest. Matthew 25:15a, NKJV, reads: "And to one he gave five talents, to another two, and to another one, to each according to his own ability" (skill or expertness in handling money). In this passage Jesus is telling a parable about an investor who entrusts his money to those who have skill in investing.

Having a hard time seeing that? Then I suggest you re-read verse 14 [with this author's additions for clarification].

v14 "For the kingdom of heaven is like a man [investor] traveling to a far country [who was busy with other things], who called his own servants [investment team] and delivered his goods [money] to them [with the purpose of increasing the investment]" (NKJV).

A side note in the above passage is the investor's wise use of diversification. Although each servant possessed the ability to provide a return based on that ability, there was no guarantee the servants would produce such returns. So, to limit and/or reduce the risk associated with investing, the investor diversified the money among his investment team to ensure the greatest possible return and smallest risk.

So let's continue with the passage to determine why ability is taken into account prior to risk.

v16 "Then he who had received the five talents went and traded with them [market], and made another five talents.
v17 "And likewise he who had received two gained two more also."

In review, the (investment team) stewards "went and traded with them." Trading runs the risk that you could lose some or all of your investment. The stewards were aware of the risk associated with trading, but their skill at trading greatly increased the likelihood of a return. The steward with one talent was more aware of the risk associated with investing than he was acquainted with his ability. Because of that thought, the steward didn't invest and thus realized no gain.

Upon discovering the steward with one talent failed to yield an increase, the investor took back his money and invested with an investor with a proven track record. Why did he do that? Well, let's look at what he saw. He saw that he received an incredible 88% return on an already large sum of money, as illustrated in the following table.

	Investment	Return	Increase (%)*
Talents	5	5	63.00%
	2	2	25.00%
	1	0	0.00%
Total	8	7	88.00%

*Divide the amount in the return column by total amount originally invested.

Ex. 1) 5 divided by 8 = .63
2) 2 divided by 8 = .25
3) 1 divided by 8 = .00

If you had an investment manager with the ability to generate a large return, wouldn't you take money from the low performance manager and give it to the higher performance manager?

Gambling vs. Investing

Remember, gambling, not investing, is based on risk. In gambling you are given odds for winning (by law). With investing your success is mainly determined by your own, or your investment manager's, ability and skill in investing. (With investing, your most important asset isn't necessarily the amount of money you invest, but your knowledge level with investments.)

Although there are investments that practically guarantee a return, because not everyone possesses a great deal of "money intelligence," many people avoid those investments and spend their money on the lottery. In more cases than not, they lose their money every time.

Summary

Financial Goals For Investing

1. Adequate Funds for Retirement
2. Additional Growth Asset Purchase
3. Additional Income
4. An Inheritance for Heirs.

Basic Levels of Investing

Others - Person or entity receiving loan determines return.
Markets - Market and economic conditions determine rate of return.
Self – Investor determines the interest rate and/or potential return.

Investment Success based on investment ability and management of risk.

Ability - Skill, expertness, or talent.
Risk - The chance for injury or loss.
Greater focus on ability than on risk increases likelihood of return. Greater focus on risk than on ability increases likelihood of loss.

Chapter 11 Producer Viewpoint: Work

Work
Others
Self

The next category of increase is work. Genesis 2:2 says, "And on the seventh day God ended his work which he had made; and he rested on the seventh day from all his work which he had made" (KJV). God shows us that work is not just a natural principle but a spiritual principle. How? The Bible teaches us that God is spirit. And the above passage tells us that God worked. Well, if God is spirit and God worked, then it's logical to conclude that work is a spiritual principle.

The Bible states in Deuteronomy 15:10 that He (God) will bless all that you set your hand to do (work). For that to happen, you must begin to see work as more than a means of acquiring money. You must see work as the vehicle that brings your imagination to reality. To gain true wealth, you must see work that way.

Simply working for money is not the way to riches. Proverbs 23:4a KJV reads, "Labor not to be rich". Working for money allows you to earn enough income to pay bills, etc., but working for money alone will not bring you wealth, because you are not using work to its fullest capability. Its fullest capability is to bring to pass what God says you can do, or become.

Working brings you what you work for. You may work for honor, or for prestige, and through working you acquire exactly what you are working for in relation to the amount and frequency of work you engage in. This determines the amount of your blessing and how soon it comes to pass.

One reason many are not wealthy is the mistake of using all of the working time working solely for money, and not spending any time working on the dream that will bring wealth. For example, my background is business and accounting. If I wanted simply money, I could rely solely on employment in those fields. However, my salary would be limited by several factors, chief being the salary range of the job. But my dream or mission is to help people attain their financial goals by providing sound advice and effective methods for managing and increasing their financial positions. There is no limit to the people I could help. By providing help and blessing to them, I'm working on the dream that will bring me wealth.

Levels of Work

Here are four levels to increase your finances in the category of work.

1) Work for Others
2) Work for Self
3) Have Others Work for You
4) Have Money Work for You

Work for Others In Matthew 20:1-16, Jesus tells a parable about laborers and a landowner, and Jesus compares them to the Kingdom of Heaven. The landowner, realizing that work yields an increase, hires laborers to work for him. And it is by their labor that he increases.

The laborers also increase by earning income. With labor comes increase, but nothing is gained through idleness. Working for others is one of the ways you can increase. This means that you use your skills and/or abilities for someone else and receive a salary, commission, or hourly wage. At this level, working for others increases you but multiplies the business owner, because your participation in the system is designed to multiply the employer's interests.

Unfortunately, most people begin their quest for wealth here and remain there (working for others). They have been convinced that this is the only way for them to prosper, and that prosperity will come faster the harder they work and the more jobs they have. Proverbs 23:4 NKJV says, "Do not overwork to be rich," because constant hard labor doesn't make you rich, it makes the people you work for rich.

Working for others does provide money and/or skill to move to the next level . . . working for self.

Work for Self Luke 12:16 NKJV states, "The ground of a certain rich man yielded plentifully." There was no mention of laborers, so this most likely meant that he worked for himself or was self-employed. Self-employment means that the worker "owns the job". You don't work for any one else but yourself. Doctors, lawyers, and several others may fall into this category. You're paid directly based on the value of your abilities to others, not based on what a company says your abilities are worth as is the case in working for someone else.

Although working at this level increases you, it doesn't guarantee wealth because the principle of multiplication is not taking place in you or anyone else. Although compensation for your abilities is desirable and you would be not be answerable to a boss, there are still some potential drawbacks to working for yourself. First and foremost, should you stop working for any reason and for any length of time, you would lose money.

Secondly, working for yourself doesn't present the opportunity for multiplication. One key to becoming wealthy and prosperous is understanding and exercising the principle of multiplication. Your goal at the self-employment level is to provide excellent service. By providing this type of service, you should attract an increase in your client base. As your client base increases, so does your workload. Then you must understand and walk in the principle of multiplication by having others work for you.

Have Others Work for You In Matthew 20:1-16, Jesus tells a parable about laborers and a landowner, who are compared to the Kingdom of Heaven. The landowner, realizing that work yields an increase, hires laborers to work for him. It is by their labor that he increases.

Finally, the principle of multiplication begins to work for you. When the work gets too great, you need to hire people to work for you. Hiring others creates a system designed to bring you wealth and to supply the system with employees whose job is to do that. Having employees also enables you to expand production and reap greater profits than you would have working alone. Your new goal is to increase production, not solely through your own efforts, but through managing the productivity of others, also. Your income and wealth would be greater and generated much faster by the effort of others. Hence, you would have multiplied your income by multiplying the efforts of others and not yourself. As your level of income increases, surplus money can multiplied by . . . having money work for you.

Have Money Work for You Matthew 25:14 states that the master embarked on a long journey and left his money with his servants. The master assigned his servants the task of putting the money to work; increasing it. The servant with one talent, however, didn't increase because he was idle or he left the talent idle. Idle money doesn't increase.

Active Money is the hardest worker I know: it works 24 hours daily, 7 days a week, etc. It never calls in sick, and money's offspring (interest) works for you, too. Employees and money are essential components of a working system designed to make you wealthy. As you contribute money to your financial plan, you are supplying the system with the means to bring you wealth. Here, the principle of multiplication comes into effect, and when it is properly applied, money will multiply itself. Investing is one opportunity afforded to you to grow your asset and/or reap an income from it.

As indicated previously, you have the potential to increase your finances. There are also Pros and Cons associated with functioning solely in one level of work.

Pros and Cons of Each Level of Work

Work for others.

Pros - Steady Income
Security
Little or no risk

Cons - Pay based on boss's evaluation of your ability
Limited earning potential
Lack of development in your non-job-related individual talent and ability
Lack of opportunity for your business to be multiplied by others.
Lack of opportunity to have money work for you

Work for Self

Pros - Pay based on abilities
Independence, freedom from answering to someone else

Cons - End of increase upon cessation of work by choice or necessity (illness)
Increased dependence on non-fixed income
Lack of opportunity for your business to be multiplied by others
Lack of opportunity to have money work for you

Others Work for You.

Pro - Finances generated for you by others

Cons - Increased government/regulatory involvement
Personal problems of employees
Risks to productivity and quality control
Increased dependence on non-fixed income

Money Works for You

Pro - Money working 24 hours/day every day

Cons - Capital Gains taxes
Amount of Capital needed to maintain standard of living and investment program

I believe that using a blend of all levels can lead to consistent and abundant financial blessing. The use of each level minimizes or eliminates the cons associated with working solely in one level. For example, working for others can provide income you need to take care of your financial obligations. With those obligations being met by your earned income and frugality, your free time can be spent discovering and honing your abilities and talents, determining how to generate money from using them to serve others. As your talent and ability improve, people will increasingly desire your services, beyond that which you can provide alone; then you can hire others to take up the additional workload, making them part of your system, all the while maintaining your source of earned income (job) if you desire. And last but not least, during any of these stages you can direct money to investments that may allow money to work for you as well.

Summary

Levels of Work
Work for Others (Be an employee)
Work for Self (Be self-employed)
Have Others Work for You (Be an employer)
Have Money Work for You (Be an investor)

Pros and Cons
Exist and differ in every level
Can be balanced by working in several levels simultaneously

Chapter 12
Financial Stewardship

Before increasing you must know where you are today so you can measure the increase. Financial Stewardship requires a total accounting of all of your assets and liabilities, income and expenses, current and year to date. Next, this information must be converted into financial ratios. Financial ratios provide an accurate assessment of your financial status. Before we record these ratios, let's define and examine each financial tool. The tools for managing and increasing money are (1) an asset, (2) income, (3) a liability, and (4) an expense.

Tools for Increase

Assets A parable in the Bible helps us consider the way we use the assets we've been given. Results from sowing in poor ground and good ground are contrasted in Matthew 13:3, 7-8 & 12 NKJV.

v3 Then He spoke many things to them in parables, saying: "Behold, a sower went out to sow.
v7 "And some fell among thorns, and the thorns sprang up and choked them.
v8 "But others fell on good ground and yielded a crop: some a hundredfold, some sixty, some thirty.
v12 "For whoever has [assets are in excess of liabilities], to him more will be given, and he will have abundance; but whoever does not have [liabilities are in excess of assets], even what he has [assets/money] will be taken away from him."

In this parable, Jesus talks about sowing the Word of God in the hearts of men. He instructs his disciples to use the principles of good farmers. He tells them the benefits of planting in good ground and the perils of planting among thorns. Like the Word of God, money is also plantable seed. If money is "planted" in a suitable investment, then it "grows". If it is "planted" in an environment or situation that doesn't encourage "growth," then the money is "choked" and eventually dwindles away. What type of farmer you are determines how you plant your seed. Good farmers plant their seed in good ground as the scripture indicates: seed planted in good ground yields a crop or increase.

"So then," I'm sure you are wondering, "what is good ground?" Good ground is something in which you can plant your seed (money) and the seed will yield an increase. The purpose of planting is to maximize seed. Good ground maximizes seed as assets grow money. In the spiritual realm, good ground is God's work, i.e., the Christ-centered ministries of God (discussed in Chapter Six). In the material realm, assets represent good ground.

What are assets? An asset is anything of economic value, owned by an individual or business, which can be converted to cash. Just like good ground, assets provide for the seed an environment needed to grow and yield a crop. For example, if you plant your money in a stock and the value of the stock increases, then your yield does what? It also increases, meaning you earn money. Why are assets so important? Imagine having a magnet in your hand and then waving your hand over some metal. What happens?

The metal is attracted to the magnet. Well, assets have the same effect on money, which is why I also refer to assets as "money magnets".

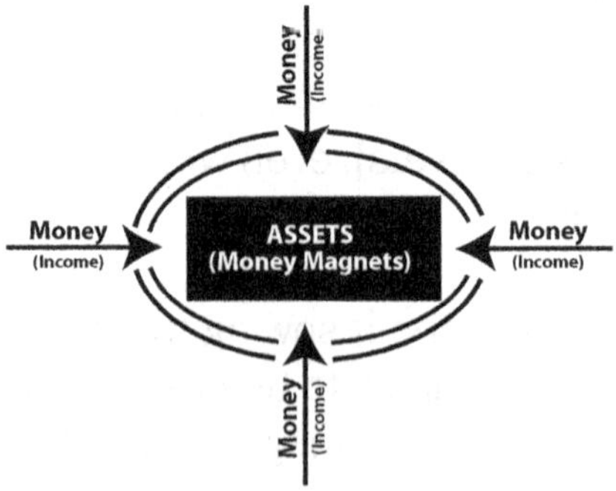

By building your finances on assets, you are following the principle of planting in good ground. Assets provide financial growth, stability, and protection from and during financial storms. Assets include cash (the money you have), Accounts Receivable (the money others owe you), bonds (the money the government and corporations owe you), stocks (ownership of a company), real estate, equipment (ownership of property), etc. Assets grow seeds through the use of money and an increase or gain in the value of non-monetary items such as stocks, bonds, and land, etc.

Use of Money Our country revolves around the use of money. Every day many Americans invest in stocks, buy things they need, or if they don't have an immediate use for money, deposit their money in banks.

Because they don't need all of their money at once, people may use their money to make more money. For example, an individual asks for a $1,000.00 loan to help fund a new business venture. You just happen to have the money in the bank, and you don't have an immediate need for it, so you decide to lend the money. After the borrower satisfies your credit requirements (perhaps by placing an item as security), you both agree in writing to the period of time the borrower will be allowed to use your money and the interest to be paid to you for the use of your money. The borrower is to make monthly payments to you for one year at a simple interest rate of 10%. The borrower is responsible for paying you $1,100.00, which represents the loan principal of $1000, plus interest amounting to $100. To you that loan is a receivable or an asset, and the interest represents the income resulting from possessing an asset.

Value of Objects Stocks represent ownership in a company. One factor contributing to the value of the stock is the profitability of the company. If the company's profits increase, the possibility of a corresponding increase in the value of the company's stock is expected. For example, let's say you purchased stock in AAA Manufacturing at $25.00. In six months the company is earning greater than expected profits. The next day the stock price increases to $50.00, meaning you've just increased your assets through the increase in value of your stock.

Original Price	New Price	Increase in Assets
$25.00	$50.00	$25.00 per share

Types of Assets

An asset is property, tangible or intangible, that is owned by and generates or potentially generates for you money, a gain, or more income than it costs to operate or own. There are three types of assets: Primary, Secondary, and Consumable.

Primary The following are examples of primary assets. Primary assets usually increase in value or can potentially provide a return.

Cash on Hand (Savings Account, CD, etc.)
Stock
Cash related Accounts
Mutual Funds
Treasury Bills, notes
Bonds
Real Estate
Annuities
Cash Value of Life Insurance Policies
Skills/Talents/Abilities

Secondary The following are examples of secondary assets. These are assets that, when properly maintained for a period of time and sold, can potentially generate income above cost.

Rare coins
Art
Stamps
Other Collectibles
Real Estate Development

Consumable The following are examples of consumable assets. These are assets whose value tends to decrease (depreciate) over the asset's useful life.

Television
Stereo
Clothes
Car
Furniture
Computer
Microwave

Consumable assets can still bring money to you if sold; however, the money generated from the sale will often not exceed the original purchase price. The reason personal property of this nature, i.e., furniture, etc., is listed as a consumable asset is that those items begin to lose value the moment you buy them. The process is called depreciation. Depreciation is a decrease in value of property through wear, deterioration, or obsolescence.

Let's say a married couple, after buying a new home, wants new furniture. They find the furniture they want for $2,000.00. Five years and two children later, the new furniture has become a makeshift trampoline to the children. Because of this, the couple decides on selling the furniture at a garage sale. They sell it to a college student for $50.00 – a far cry from the purchase price of $2,000.00. The furniture was actually a consumable asset, because the couple derived no income from it, i.e., cost $2,000.00 minus selling price $50.00 equals $1,950.00 loss.

Income.

Income results from planting seed in good ground. Continuing the analogy of money as seed, and assets as good ground, then what do you reap from sowing seeds in good ground? Fruit. Income is that fruit. Income is money or value realized from work, investments, and/or services and products provided. Income is an inflow of cash, a derivative of assets.

In other words, income is what assets or "money magnets" attract. Because assets increase in value and provide a return on money, realized and/or unrealized value results. Unrealized value is an increase in the value of an asset that is not sold to receive the increase as income. Realized value is an increase in the value of an asset that is sold so the owner receives the increase as income.

There are three types of income. They are passive, earned, and service/product. Passive Income is received from non-active involvement investing. Earned Income is received from employment in a business. Service/Product Income is received from providing a service or product to customers.

How Do You Increase Income? You increase income by increasing the price of the services and/or products provided. You increase income by providing additional priced products and services. You increase income by deriving interest from passive investments (real estate, stocks, etc.). You increase income by earnings from additional employment or by a salary increase. You increase income by selling an asset. You prepare to increase income by purchasing income-producing assets.

Net Income is the amount of money remaining after subtracting all expenses from income. Without net income in personal finances, people live "from paycheck to paycheck". Their income doesn't exceed their expenses. Net Income (or lack of net income) is evidence. It is evidence of the state of an individual's personal finances.

(I)ncome - (E)xpenses = (N)et (I)ncome

How to Ensure Net Income Net Income grows when you increase income in relation to expenses. Net Income grows when you maintain income and decrease expenses. Net Income grows when you increase appreciable assets and decrease liabilities.

A good farmer ensures net income and/or continued net income by using income (seeds) to purchase appreciable assets and not excessive liabilities. Good farmers use their surplus to purchase more assets (plant in good ground) because they know that if they purchase more assets, their income will increase proportionately. (See diagram.)

Tools for Decrease

Liabilities and expenses are tools for decrease. Planting your seed among thorns is a way to reap decrease. Look again at Matthew 13:3, 7-8 & 12.

v3 Then He spoke many things to them in parables, saying: "Behold, a sower went out to sow.
v7 "And some fell among thorns, and the thorns sprang up and choked them.
v8 "But others fell on good ground and yielded a crop: some a hundredfold, some sixty, some thirty.
v12 "For whoever has [assets are in excess of liabilities], to him more will be given, and he will have abundance; but whoever does not have [liabilities are in excess of assets], even what he has [assets/money] will be taken away from him."

Liabilities Let's review. We've learned that money is seed. We've also learned that assets in the material realm represent good ground and that income represents the fruit resulting from planting in good ground.

To give his disciples a well-rounded view of kingdom farming, Jesus taught them what would happen if they planted their seeds among thorns. He taught them that thorns choke seeds. And, if money represents seeds, then following the same analogy, there are things in which you can plant your money that will choke it and prevent it from growing. Those thorns are called liabilities. To put it simply, liabilities are debt.

By building your liabilities, you are following the principle of planting among thorns. And thorns do what to seeds? They choke the life out of them. Liabilities are "money repellants"; they repel money away from you.

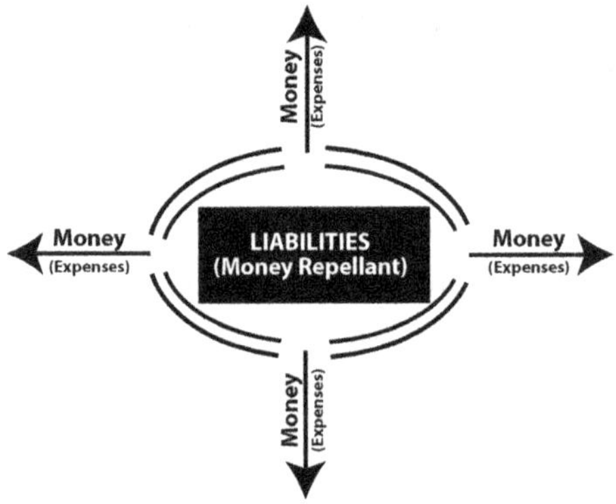

Examples of liabilities include mortgage, personal loans, credit card debt, auto loans, school loans, etc. Liabilities grow when you purchase things you can't afford, and when you buy them on credit instead of using cash. Liabilities grow when money is spent on things which don't grow in value.

Purchases on Credit You go to the mall, and you see an outfit that you must have. But you don't have the money. What to do? What to do? Yes!! You have your credit card. Just whip it out and charge it!!

Congratulations, you just increased your liabilities. The liability is called accounts payable. Accounts payable means the use of credit to purchase non-income producing or non-guaranteed value increasing items.

Let me know if these sound familiar: clothes, cars, jewelry, furniture, movies, video games, music CD's, etc. By purchasing the outfit on credit, you enabled the retailer to earn income from the outfit or asset. And you have decreased your money by adding the new liability. "Well," you might say, "how did the retailer earn money from an asset and I purchase a liability with the same item?" I'm sure you believe you purchased an asset, because you can sell the outfit later for money. Yes, that is true to a degree. But remember, the retailer included a markup on the sale. When and if you resell, you will on average receive only a fraction of the purchase amount.

Check out your local consignment shop, and you will see for yourself. A dress or suit originally purchased at $500, and sold to a consignment shop, may bring you on average only $30-50, well short of its original price.

Items That Don't Grow in Value Everything purchased is either an asset or a liability. By purchasing things that don't normally grow in value, you increase the number of liabilities you have. This happens when you purchase non-income producing or non-guaranteed value increasing items, whether purchased with cash or on credit.

Do these sound familiar: clothes, cars, jewelry, furniture, movies, video games, Music CD's, etc.? We like them, don't we? I know that I do. Several of the items mentioned can have great sentimental value, like perhaps an engagement ring or expensive car, but sentimental value doesn't help you reach your financial goals -- financial independence, for example. If we purchase or rent too many of these items, what happens? Money begins to be repelled from us. Why? Because we spent more money on items that repel money than on items that attract money.

A liability is something owed, or something owned that generates either no income or more expense to operate to own. The following are examples of liabilities:

House Mortgage
Car/Auto/Consumer/School Loan
Credit Card
Some Personal Property

Some of you might challenge the listing of a house mortgage as a liability, but if you have a mortgage, you don't own the house, the bank does. The banks provide the opportunity of home ownership, and they charge you for that opportunity. The charge is the interest you pay in addition to the principal or loan amount. You repay the loan with interest, and then you own the house.

Remember my definition of an asset: an asset (something that attracts money) is property – tangible or intangible – that is owned and generates either a gain, or more income than it costs to operate or own.

Expenses Just as income is what planting in good ground yields, an expense is what planting among thorns yields. Expenses are items charged against income and cause an outflow of cash. Expenses consume income and reduce net worth. They pull away your fruit. Matthew 13:12 NKJV says, "But whoever does not have [assets are fewer than liabilities], even what he has [money] will be taken away from him." Expenses are created as you increase liabilities. Expenses can include utilities, taxes, entertainment, food, clothes, auto loan payments, mortgage payments, credit card payments, etc. Expenses are a part of life. However, we must be careful not to allow expenses to grow and consume more of income than is necessary.

How Do You Increase Expenses? Expenses grow when you experience increased cost of producing products and providing services. Expenses grow when you increase consumption. Expenses grow when you experience increased cost for maintaining lifestyle (houses, car, clothes, etc.).

Acquisition of assets, liabilities, income, and expenses contributes to whether or not we generate a profit in our personal financial lives.

Net Loss. Net Loss is revealed when, after subtracting expenses from income, there is no money left and expenses remain. This can cause serious problems. A person who covers only costs, with no net income, is in dire straits and needs to change to ensure survivability.

If you are working, and your working yields only enough to barely survive, then your planting process must change, because if you continue the status quo, then the only people who will benefit from your work will be your company, the government, and your creditors. The person who needs to benefit most from working, doesn't. That person is you. Your wages will bring no net income with which to fund your personal dreams and goals. The net income must be there to provide seeds for planting in the future.

How to Ensure a Net Loss

Loss grows when you increase expenses in relation to income. Loss grows when you maintain expenses and decrease income. Loss grows when you increase liabilities and decrease assets.

An individual ensures loss and/or continued loss by using income to purchase liabilities and not assets. People with means, who don't possess "the knowledge of wealth," use their surplus to purchase more liabilities because they don't know that if they buy more liabilities, their expenses will increase proportionately. (See diagram.)

Tools for Revealing the Status Quo

Balance Sheet Your assets and liabilities are recorded on a balance sheet. A balance sheet is divided into two columns. The total sum of your assets is placed on the left side, while your liabilities are listed on the right. The balance sheet shows the total of assets, liabilities, and Net Worth. Net Worth is what is left after figuring total assets minus total liabilities.

(+)Assets (-) Liabilities (=) Total Net Worth

These figures can have a direct effect on your income statement. Assets tend to increase income while liabilities increase expenses. If you don't seem to be increasing, compare your personal possessions to the asset list and liability list earlier in the chapter. Of which do you have more, assets or liabilities? If you answered assets, then what type of assets do you have? Most people have consumable assets. Consumable assets are the least beneficial of all assets because 1) they depreciate, 2) many people usually incur liabilities to acquire them, and 3) the liabilities generate expenses.

Income Statement Your income and expenses are recorded on an income statement. An income statement is divided into top and bottoms halves on a sheet of paper. Monthly Income is recorded and totaled on the top half, and expenses are recorded and totaled on the bottom half. Total monthly expenses are then subtracted from total monthly income. If total monthly income is greater than total monthly expenses, then a Net Income is the result. If total expenses are greater than total income, then Net Loss is the result.

(+) Income (-) Expenses (=) Equals Net Income (+) or Loss (-)

Congratulations! You have probably created your first financial statements. Now, what do you do with them? How do you determine if you are progressing financially or need to make some changes?

Financial Ratios Use what are called Financial Ratios. These ratios measure your financial performance. There are four ratios we'll consider in this section: Solvency, Liquidity, Savings, and Debt Service Ratios.

Solvency Ratio. T(otal) a(ssets) ÷ T(otal) d(ebts) = Solvency Ratio

This ratio determines the extent to which your existing assets would be able to satisfy your total debts if necessary. Your ability to completely satisfy your debts with your existing assets is called solvency. A good solvency ratio is one in which your assets equal or exceed your liabilities, i.e., your stocks, bonds, and home value exceed your school loan, mortgage, credit balance, etc.

Let's take an example of a fictional young couple A, who have $50,000 in assets and $10,000 in debt. Their Solvency Ratio would look like this:

Total Assets (divided by) Total Debts = Ratio
$50,000 (divided by) $10,000 = 5.00

This couple would have to experience a 500% decline in their assets before they would be considered insolvent. Our young couple's ratio is excellent.

The same can't be said for young couple B who have $10,000 in assets and $50,000 in debt. Their Solvency Ratio would look like this:

Total Assets (divided by) Total Debts = Ratio
$10,000 ÷ $50,000 = 0.20

This couple is technically insolvent. If their creditors called for immediate payment of all their debt, they would not have sufficient assets to repay. Even after selling everything they own, they would be able to repay only 20% of their debts.

A ratio that is 1 or greater indicates solvency. A ratio less than 1 can be an indication of problems.

Liquidity Ratio Liquid Assets ÷ Monthly Expenses = Ratio

This ratio determines the extent to which your current liquid assets (cash and cash equivalents) would be able to satisfy your total monthly expenses in the event your monthly income were interrupted.

Using the following information on couple A from the example above, we can calculate the Liquidity Ratio.

Cash on hand $1,000	Mortgage $1,000
Savings Account $2,000	Car Payment $ 700
Money Market $2,000	Utilities $1,000

Liquid Assets ÷ Monthly Expenses = Liquidity Ratio
$5,000 (divided by) $2,700 = 1.85

In the event of a loss of income, couple A would be able to pay their monthly expenses for nearly 2 (1.85) months from their existing liquid assets. Conventional financial planning calls for a minimum ratio of 3 or higher. Your level of job security and insurance coverage against loss from other situations could enable you to be comfortable with a lower ratio.

Savings Ratio Annual Savings ÷ Gross Income = Savings Ratio

This ratio determines the extent to which you save a portion of your income. Conventional financial planning calls for a savings ratio range of 8-20%. Once you reach your liquidity ratio goals, your options are no longer limited to placing this savings in a liquid asset; stocks, bonds, and mutual funds are all attractive alternatives.

Let's take another example of fictional young couple A who have $800 in annual savings and earn an annual gross income of $40,000. Their Savings Ratio would look like this:

Total Annual Savings (divided by) Total Gross Income = Income Ratio
$800 ÷ $40,000 = 0.02

This couple's savings are only 2% of their gross income. Taking other factors, such as the amount of money available in relation to their expenses and liabilities outstanding, into account, they are not saving enough money in comparison to their gross income. A ratio that is .08 or greater indicates a healthy rate of savings. A ratio less than .08 can be an indication of potential financial problems.

Debt Service Ratio Total Monthly Loan Payments ÷ Monthly Gross Income = Ratio

This ratio determines what percentage of your income is spent monthly on debt repayment. The greater the percentage spent on debt repayment, the less is available for savings, investing, and giving.

Using the information from the previous example, we can calculate the debt service ratio for couple A.

Mortgage $1,000   Car Payment $ 700
Total Loan Payments=$1,700
Annual Income $100,000/12 months=$8333.33
Total Monthly Loan Payments (divided by) Monthly Gross Income = Debt Service Ratio
$1,700 (divided by) $8333.33 = .20 or 20%

Couple A spends approximately 20% of their gross monthly income on debt repayments. This falls well within the acceptable range of 0-37%. If Couple A's ratio had exceeded 37%, then they would have needed to concentrate their efforts toward debt reduction.

So," you are probably saying, "what's the big deal about these ratios, anyway?"

Let me share a personal testimony with you on how important they are to analyzing your financial health. A client of mine (I'll call her Laura) and I were creating her financial statements. Her focus was primarily on the income statement, because she experienced a financial surplus (based on the information she provided). She thought, because she had enough money to pay her debts and regular monthly bills, she was doing ok financially. She hadn't taken the financial ratios into account. The first ratio I calculated for her was the savings ratio. Her savings ratio revealed that on an annual basis she saved less than 1% of her annual gross salary. This indicated that, although she could afford to pay her debt (the major concern of most people), she didn't pay herself an adequate wage (savings). She was consistently paying out 99% of her annual gross income. 99%!!! In layperson's terms, that means 99% of her money was flowing out of her hands into the hands of other people.

For whom was she working, herself or the bill collector? Amazed yet? If not, then look at the following startling revelation.

If Laura earns $20,000 annually and continues to work for a total of 30 years with no change in salary, then after working 30 years she will earn a total of $600,000 (30 x $20,000). Let's also say that Laura doesn't change her savings habits over this period of time. If she consistently saves 1% of her annual gross salary (excluding interest), as she does currently, then she will be in for a rude awakening 30 years down the road, because she will have only $6,000. Multiplying her annual salary by her annual savings rate ($20,000 x .01) equals annual savings. Then multiply this figure ($200) by 30 years to arrive at $6,000. How would you feel if after 30 years of hard work you had saved only $6,000?

Had Laura saved 10% of her annual income, as is usually recommended in Financial Planning, then she would have ended up with $60,000, not taking into account any potential interest earned from investments, resulting in an even greater amount of return. That is ten times as much as she was on course to have if she didn't change. As you can imagine, she was shocked that her current savings or lack of savings would have such an impact on her future. Immediately she asked me to help her create an action plan.

Improving Your Balance

Once your self-assessment has been performed, you are probably curious about how to improve your financial balance. Here are some actions that will improve your balance.

1) Tithe.
2) Save a portion of income for yourself.
3) Reduce idle desire expenses and/or review living expenses.
4) Give (to ministries & charities).
5) Invest (put your money to work for you).
6) Reduce liabilities.
7) Work on improving your ability to generate additional income.

The first four actions to improve your financial balance were mentioned in an earlier chapter, but I can't stress their importance enough. Tithing, saving, and giving move you to the realm of provider, while gaining a handle on "desire" expenses presents more money for the provider realm. But why are these three so important?

Before I answer that, there are two Bible verses I would like to present. Proverbs 12:24-25 NKJV states:

v24a There is one who scatters, yet increases more.
The author is saying there are some who (provide) money, yet they receive more money.
v24b And there is one who withholds more than is right, but it leads to poverty.
The author is saying there are some who withhold money from God, themselves (savings), and others, to spend on their desires, and this action leads to poverty. The author goes on to say in verse 25 that the generous soul will be made rich because he who waters (gives) will also be watered (given to).
It looks like this:

God
You$-----> Savings----------->You$$
Others

Spiritual law describes God's blessing as rewarding your "watering" (provision) by watering and increasing you in turn. As your generosity increases, your return increases, increasing your inflow. I will expand briefly on three other verses with a more detailed exploration in the chapter on Increase.

Putting your money to work means taking available (idle) money and investing in something or someone with the goal of regaining your principal with a return on your investment. For you all who think it's too late to begin investing, your money can still be productive, despite the fact people are saying, "If you're not in the stock market or actively investing, it is too late to realize good returns." Investing improves your balance by adding to your short term (inflow) and long term (assets) financial statements – income statements and balance sheets, respectively.

Putting your money to work also includes using a portion of idle funds to reduce liabilities. The reduction of liabilities also causes an eventual reduction in expenses once the debt is paid. This improves your balance because this reduction in liabilities increases the percentage of assets in relation to your net worth and provides additional available income due to the reduction in expenses.

Lastly, you must work on improving your ability to generate finances. Remember the parable of stewardship. Each steward received money (talents) according to his or her ability. With that firmly established, you can improve your position by perfecting your abilities, thereby increasing the amount of money you receive.

Maintaining your Balance

Budget The establishment and maintenance of a budget is a key component to managing your funds. As discussed in previous chapters, budgets serve a two-fold purpose: They determine where you are and help you determine where you are going. By using your budget as a guideline, you are better able to monitor your balances.

Regularly compare your actual monthly income and expense with your established budget. If your comparisons reveal a category or categories in your actual column that are causing an imbalance, you can then determine why and adjust your actual income/expense accordingly.

Although a great portion of this section has been spent on budgeting, there are three other essential components to maintaining your balance. They are: time, attention, and effort.

Time The first essential component to maintaining your balance is time. Time used wisely is repeatedly cited as one important factor of successful people. Who among us has become a champion athlete, an accomplished speaker, or other successful person without the wise use of time? Without using time wisely to perfect their art, craft, skill, and/or abilities, they could not achieve their established goals.

This principle also applies to the management balance of your finances. Time must be used not only to understand your budget, but also to create and understand financial statements, to review data, to compare data, and to complete a host of other activities essential in your management balance. The amount of time used for this purpose will be reflected in your financial management balance. Remember, you reap what you sow. If you sow time in managing your money, you reap the benefits of managed money. Time invested in managing finances reaps benefits, and these benefits are compounded when teamed with attention and effort.

Attention Let's use an example of two athletes in training. One uses time daily to practice and hone his talent. The other athlete combines time with attention to the way he trains. They train the same way until #2 notices that by changing his technique he can gain far greater results. So, now although they spend the same amount of time training, because #2 paid attention to what he was doing and noticed something that could improve, now he reaps greater benefits from his time.

Effort This same athlete began observing problems in his body. By taking the effort to observe what he ate, how he slept, etc., he was able to solve the problem.

Paying attention to budgets and their relationship with income and expenses helps you refine and improve your financial position. By the same token, effort expended gathering information and correcting any imbalance helps to determine how well and how quickly a problem is solved or an opportunity is used to advantage.

Exercises

1. Below is a sample list of Assets and Liabilities. Using this list as a guide, create your own list from your financial transactions over the past three years. Have you acquired more assets or more liabilities?

Assets	Liabilities
Stocks	Auto Loan
Bonds	Personal Loan
Real Estate	Pest Control
Savings Account	Rent to Own
Mutual Funds	Mortgage
Loans	Credit Card
Annuities	Cable TV
Gold	School Loan
CDs	Phone
IRA	Water

2. Using your list, which liabilities can you reduce or eliminate?

Summary

Assets are money magnets. They attract money.
Liabilities are money repellant. They repel money.
Net Income results when income exceeds expenses.
Net Loss results when expenses exceed income.

Chapter 13
Starting Your Journey

Where Are You?

Before your financial journey begins you must determine where you are and what tools are available to transport you to your destination. You must ask yourself questions such as:

a) "What do I have to save that I may increase?"
b) "What can I give which will assist me to increase?"
c) "What can I invest in myself, others, business, markets, etc.?"
d) "Am I willing to work for an increase?"

These questions play an important role in the success or failure of your financial journey. They help you see where you stand in regard to your current station in life. To begin in the realm of increase, you must perform the self-analysis on "where you are" in terms of increase. This means identifying how you feel spiritually (spiritual), how you think (mental), how your friends feel about you (social), and how you feel emotionally about increase (emotional).

Many publications cite that we are what we think, which is partially true. It's my belief that we as human beings are composed of and act based not only on what we think but on three additional factors: spiritual, social, and emotional. Let's spend some time reviewing each.

Spiritual Once Jesus Christ has renewed our spiritual lives, we have the choice to live an abundant life or one revolving around poverty. In determining if we want to increase, we must begin with our innermost core–our spiritual worship–to determine if our spiritual lives are based on the principles of abundance or on the principles of poverty. Our relationship with God places us in contact with Him who is abundance. Unfortunately, there are those of us who, for whatever reason, fail to see the abundance of God available to us and, by default, lead lives based on lack.

Many of those beliefs can be traced to teachings emphasizing "godliness" at the expense of abundance. Those who believe this cite scriptures like Proverbs 13:7 NKJV, which states, "There is one who makes himself rich, yet has nothing; And one who makes himself poor, yet has great riches."

Another such scripture is found in Matthew 19:21, 23 NKJV, which reads as follows: "Jesus said to him [the rich young ruler], 'If you want to be perfect, go, sell what you have and give to the poor, and you will have treasure in heaven, and come, follow me. . . . Assuredly, I say to you that it is hard for a rich man to enter the kingdom of heaven.'"

The interpretation of these scriptures to teach that God wants us poor is inaccurate. God says in His Word that we can have both godliness and abundance.

In reviewing the scripture in Proverbs, we see that the author says there is one who makes himself rich, yet has nothing; and one who makes himself poor, yet has great riches. Those possessing the "poverty mentality" may read the scriptures this way: Everyone who makes himself rich really has nothing, and everyone who makes himself poor has great riches (spirituality). Those possessing the "abundance mind" discern the author's meaning, which is that your financial status does not directly affect your possession of true riches (Heaven). I believe that God is saying that your possession of riches doesn't guarantee Heaven or Hell and that your lack of riches doesn't prevent you from going to Heaven or Hell.

The way you interpreted the above passage could give insight into your personal belief about increase. There may be some of you who are still not convinced about the true meaning of the passage. Read Proverbs

13:22 NKJV. It reads, "A good man leaves an inheritance to his children's children, But the wealth of the sinner is stored up for the righteous." Wait a minute!! According to the "poverty mind," verse 7 says you can't have Heaven and be rich. So, how can a good man leave an inheritance to his children's children? Poor people usually leave debt to their children.

If we continue in the verse, we find further evidence disputing the proof stated by the "poverty mind." "The wealth of the sinner is laid up for the just" (KJV).

Why? To keep us out of Heaven (as believed by the "poverty mind")? No, to give us a means to take care of our responsibilities and perpetuate the gospel (Deuteronomy 8:18). Need just a little more convincing? Remember Matthew 19:23? Well, I'm sure the "poverty mind" people do, too. The clarification is found in Matthew's words in verse 22, which reads: "But when the young man heard that saying [v.21], he went away sorrowful, for he had great possessions." So that's the reason for Jesus' statement in verse 23? Nope, the other piece of the answer is there. Jesus said to him, "If you want to be perfect [stand out boldly], go, sell what you have and give to the poor, and you will have treasure in heaven; and come, follow Me."

The "poverty mind" reads the scripture this way: Go, sell [all] that you have and give [it all] to the poor [that you may be poor], and you will have treasure in heaven; and [once you are poor] come, follow Me."

Why would Jesus want the rich young man to sell all and become poor? The scriptures clearly say that Jesus became poor that we could be rich (2 Corinthians 8:9). The "abundant mind" hears this: "Go, sell what you have [on hand] and give [the proceeds] to the poor [that you may learn first hand that giving is the way of the Lord], and you will have treasure in heaven [because you will have learned and followed God's way], and come [once the principle of giving is learned], follow Me" ["For where your treasure is, there will your heart be also" {Matthew 6:21, Luke 12:34, KJV}]. Do you see the difference? Do you see why the young rich ruler was so sorrowful? It was because he was selfish/greedy. He wasn't willing to share his abundance with the poor.

Giving is a prerequisite if you want to possess abundance and follow Christ. Christ knew that selfishness in the realm of money/possessions leads to the evil as stated in 1 Timothy 6:10 NKJV: "For the love of money is a root of all kinds of evil, for which some have strayed from the faith in their greediness, and pierced themselves through with many sorrows."

Once it is determined how you worship, whether in abundance or in poverty, the next realm must be reviewed. Because the objective of this book is to share well-rounded views of finance, I will proceed as if you chose "abundantly".

Mental So, you've decided that your spiritual life and worship will be through abundance. Then, your next step is to ensure that your mind is renewed with abundant thoughts, which lead to abundant thinking. Then, you must examine your thinking to ensure it agrees with abundant life and worship. For example, there are people who through abundant worship desire miracles, money, and healing. Many, however, don't experience these and other results of abundant worship because their thinking doesn't match their spiritual life and worship. Remember, when we accept Jesus, we become His siblings. We have this in common, that we spiritually worship God. Jesus stated to the Children of Israel (and us) in John 10:10 "The thief does not come except to steal, and to kill, and to destroy. I have come that they [you] may have life, and that they may have it more abundantly" (NKJV).

According to the verse, Jesus came that we would experience abundant living and worship now. Since this is the case, what hinders us from receiving what Jesus freely gives? I believe the answer is found in Proverbs 23:7 KJV, which states: "As [a man] thinketh in his heart, so is he." The author of Proverbs is saying that whatever a man thinks about, he will become or experience.

Thoughts are the root of many of the conditions you are experiencing in life. Those thoughts usually come from three sources:

1) Our Senses (what we hear/see, etc.)
2) The Devil
3) God.

Examples of these thoughts are as follows:
a) Senses - "I've been poor all my life."
b) Devil - "I've been poor and will always be poor."
c) God - "I've been poor, but Jesus died that I might be rich."

Which thoughts are you hearing in your mind? Be honest.

If the above scenario (whatever a man thinks about, he will become or experience) applies to you, the thought that you constantly hear in your mind is the reality you will experience. Thinking God-inspired thoughts leads directly to positive belief. Once belief is established, then faith is sure to follow. A simple way to determine if God or the Devil inspired a thought is to analyze the results. If the thought filled you with hope, it was God-inspired, because He brings hope to all situations, especially hopeless ones. If the thought took away the hope you had, causing you to doubt yourself or God, then it was Devil- inspired.

Throughout the New Testament, Jesus asked people if they believed they could be healed. The woman with the issue of blood said to herself (thought), "If only I may touch His clothes, I shall be made well" (Mark 5:28, NKJV). Her thinking and acting on a God-inspired thought yielded hope, increased belief, and ultimately faith, and she received a miracle. So, how do you think like God? Renew your mind with His Word. By renewing your mind with His Word, you immerse yourself in the Words inspired by the mind of God. The more you reaffirm your mind with His Word, the more frequently and easily His thoughts will come to you. His thoughts will inspire and encourage you to greatness.

Social/Friends You are now on the right track. You desire the abundant life, your thoughts are in line with what you desire. Nothing can stop you, right? Unfortunately, yes, something can, if left unchecked.

As you renew your mind with God's Word, you must be careful of the amount of time you spend with certain people. Why? As your thinking elevates, people whose thoughts aren't elevated will (often unknowingly) do their best to convince you that you are setting your goals too high. In addition, they say that no one has accomplished what you are seeking to accomplish and no one will [translation: I don't believe that you can accomplish your goal]. It's been my experience that you would benefit by being led by whatever belief systems you possess that encourage you toward a worthwhile goal and/or the inspirational and encouraging words of the Word of God, not the projected belief system of someone who doesn't believe in you.

We are human beings, and a great number of us (Christian and Non-Christian alike) have un-renewed minds in certain areas and minds which can be influenced by such negative thought. Negative thought breeds negative talk. Negative talk breeds negative results. As you listen to negative talk (we can be very susceptible to words), something happens: you don't feel as confident or sure of success. That person has placed a seed of doubt in your mind.

One way to combat this is to limit or eliminate the time you spend with people who don't have renewed minds, especially in the area where you are trying to prosper, in this case your finances.

Words have power, for the scripture says in Proverbs 18:21 NKJV, "Death and life are in the power of the tongue." So, if someone is speaking death on and to you (poverty, sickness, fear, etc., then you must not dwell in his or her presence. You should spend more time and effort with those who speak life to you. Both types of people can have an effect on the Stewardship Model.

Emotional How do you really feel about growing wealthy? I'm sure many of you would say that you aren't afraid of becoming wealthy. However, growing wealthy and becoming wealthy are two different states of being. Those who fear growing wealthy spend more money on the lottery than on investments. No one is afraid to become wealthy by winning something or having God drop a million dollars in his or her lap, because this requires no effort or real courage on the individual's part.

But many don't invest their money because they are afraid of growing wealthy. Sure, some say that the risk for investing is too great, that they don't want to lose their money, but they lose money every week in the lottery, yet they continue to play. Why? I believe the answer is fear, fear of accumulating real wealth.

Subconsciously, they know that it is virtually impossible to win the lottery, thereby providing a self-fulfilling prophecy of not being able to accumulate wealth. It was fear that prevented the wicked steward from accumulating money. Instead of using his talents to accumulate money or at least putting the money in a savings account, he used an avenue in which it was impossible to increase his money (he put it in a hole). Some people today do the same thing, but the hole their fears drive them to put their money into is gambling and other get-rich-quick ventures. There have been several studies done which prove this point. There is more money spent on the lottery by those living in lower economic neighborhoods than by those living in higher economic neighborhoods. The individuals living in the higher economic neighborhoods are willing to take a minimal risk at becoming wealthy while growing wealthy. On the other hand, those individuals on the lower economic side risk a much greater percentage of their money on trying to become wealthy and little or none on growing wealthy.

How do you feel about God? Do your feelings about Him invoke happiness and joy? Do you feel the love of your Heavenly Father as He helps you accomplish your goals? Or do you feel fear and intimidation? As the lazy steward proved by example, if you are afraid of God, you will probably be afraid to do, or doubt you could do, the work He commissioned you to do. Fear paralyzes you and prevents you from acting.

Where Are You Going?

It is obvious that if you plan on going somewhere, you must know where you are going. Traveling to a destination you've visited before is easy, because you know the way. However, traveling to a brand new place, one you've never visited before, will require directions or a map. In the realm of increase, that map is called Imagination.

Imagination is the act or power of forming mental images of what is not actually present. We see examples of imagination every day: computers, televisions, telephones, etc. At one time or another these and other items like them did not exist -- physically. These items were created first by forming mental images of them, even though they didn't physically exist. Jesus encourages us in Mark 11:24 NKJV, "Whatever things you ask when you pray, believe that you receive them, and you will have them." In Matthew 17: 20 NKJV Jesus encouraged his disciples (and us), "for assuredly, I say to you, if you have faith as a mustard seed . . . nothing will be impossible for you." Paul, in Romans 4:17 NKJV, offers further encouragement from the source of creativity: "God . . . calls those things which do not exist as though they did."

These scriptures speak of two properties of imagination:

1) What you have in your heart (thoughts and feelings) leads to imagination.
2) Once you begin to do (work toward) what you imagined, nothing will be restrained from you.

The latter property is where so many in the Body of Christ fall. Based on what is in their thoughts and feelings, they already have financial prosperity. The problem is, they don't do what they imagine, and because they don't, everything they imagine is restrained from them. Imagination then becomes something from which it is distinctly different: a fairy tale. To prevent this from happening, you must know how to get where you desire financially.

Self-Assessment Questions

Am I imagining?

Am I doing what I imagine?

How Will You Get There?

So far in this chapter I've discussed where you are and where you are going. Now, we'll discuss how to get there. In review, an analysis of your thoughts, social climate, emotions, and spirit all contribute to identifying where you are. As discussed previously, imagination is the vehicle by which you determine where you are going. Finally, your actions, goals, and plans (what you're going to do and your objectives) determine how you get there.

As human beings, we all have the capability of achieving anything we imagine. As children of the Most High, we have a distinct advantage over people in the world. This advantage is found in Deuteronomy 28:8 NKJV, which states, "The Lord will command the blessing [prosperity] on you in your storehouses and in all to which you set your hand, and He will bless you in the land which the Lord your God is giving you." Isn't that wonderful? The Lord will command those things to happen in our favor.

Unfortunately, there are some who hear that scripture and will begin to do, without the benefit of planning and goal setting. A plan is any detailed method, formulated beforehand, for doing or making something. A goal is an object or end that one strives to attain. The proper order for the way to get there is:

Goal—>Plan—–>Action—–>Results

Your imagination leads to your goals. Once your goals are established, a detailed plan will assist you in determining the action needed to fulfill your goals.

Improving your balance In improving your balance you must ask yourself this question: "In which, if any, category of increase am I increasing now?" Once that is determined, you must find out if that increase is at the expense of the other categories, i.e., are you increasing so much in the savings category because you are taking monies from giving, or vice versa? Observing and following the principle of each category lets you experience true increase. If you are experiencing an imbalance, you must find out why so that you may improve.

a) Make sure your money is being managed properly.
b) Review how your money is being allocated currently.
c) Allocate your time and money so that as you increase in one category the others benefit also.

Maintain your Balance The key to maintaining your balance is the realization that no individual area of increase is greater in importance than the sum of the whole. Saving that you may experience growth in wealth is wonderful, but what good is your growth when others don't benefit? God's programs don't benefit, and you don't benefit, as illustrated by the parable of the rich fool in Luke 12:16-20 and summarized in Luke 12:21 NKJV, "So is he who lays up treasure for himself, and is not rich toward God." The same goes for giving. Giving so that God's programs and His people may benefit is good. In 2 Corinthians 8:12 NKJV encourages us, "For if there is first a willing mind, it is accepted according to what one has, and not according to what he does not have." Planning and giving is encouraged in 2 Corinthians 9:7-8 NKJV, "So let each one give as he purposes in his heart, not grudgingly or of necessity; for God loves a cheerful giver. And God is able to make all grace abound toward you, that you, always having all sufficiency in all things, may have an abundance for every good work." What good is diligence alone when it doesn't build wealth, or help God's program, etc.? When too much importance is placed on any category individually, then negative results may occur. Excess saving can lead to hoarding. Excess giving can lead to irresponsibility. Paul cautioned in 1 Timothy 5:8 NKJV, "But if anyone does not provide for his own, and especially for those of his household, he has denied the faith and is worse than an unbeliever." Excess work can lead to workaholism. Excess focus on investing can lead to greed. To maintain your balance, you must review your financial goals consistently. When you have no financial goals, or they are infrequently reviewed, then other temptations and challenges may arise. Because there's no goal, you're more easily thrown off course.

Management Proverbs The purpose of a proverb, as defined by Solomon, the author of Proverbs, is to know wisdom and instruction; to perceive the words of understanding; to receive the instruction of wisdom, justice, judgment, and equity; to give prudence to the simple; to give the young man knowledge and discretion; to increase learning of wise men; and to assist an understanding man to attain wise counsel. For the purpose of this book, I have blended the original purpose and applied it to financial management, arriving at the following:

The purpose of Financial Management Proverbs is to help all who listen attain wise counsel by receiving financial management instructions of giving, saving, spending and debt paying with the goal of giving prudence to the simple, knowledge and discretion to the young, and increased learning to the wise.

1) The tithe opens the windows of heaven; our actions afterward affect what we reap while the windows are being opened.
2) Tithe because you love God, Save because you love yourself, Give because you love others.
3) Tithing brings blessing from God, spending brings things from people.
4) Give and it shall be given to you.
5) Give in secret, receive in public.
6) He who has no financial destination makes no financial progress. Many people today don't have specific financial goals. Without specific goals people tend not to increase financially.
7) He who lives above his means will have nothing; he who lives beneath his means will have great wealth.
8) He who spends like there is no tomorrow saves like there is only today.
9) Save and increase, consume and decrease.
10) He who saves will never be broke, and he who is broke will never save.
11) Money is but an extension of the one who possesses it.
12) He who plans his finances is in control; he who is in control is free.
13) Worry consumes, faith produces. Worrying about money takes your focus off thinking of ways to generate money.

14) He who spends less need not settle for less.
15) A budget tells us what we can't afford. A goal keeps us from buying it anyway.

Increase Proverbs.

1) Worry consumes, faith produces.
2) Give and it shall be given unto you.
3) Diligent hands make you rich.
4) He who gathers by labor will increase.

Read six proverbs twice daily for one month, then move on to the next six until you complete all nineteen proverbs. Then the principles contained within these proverbs will become a part of you. Allowing these proverbs to become part of you is extremely important. By allowing these proverbs to become a part of you, you will learn to seek techniques for management of money, and increasing wealth will be second nature. It has been my experience with people that we don't always do what is best for us, but we always do what is a part of us. Be honest, many of us are overweight, or are constantly eating in unhealthy ways, yet we continue to do so. So, my telling you to save 10% of your money means nothing if saving money doesn't become a part of you.

God's viewpoint of Stewardship is designed to prosper all of us. It's our responsibility and duty to walk in the principles He has set for us. The Stewardship Model is an effective tool in assisting us in our quest to become faithful stewards with our abilities and our finances. And remember, the principles I have highlighted in this book are available to you in your quest for freedom from debt, poor spending, lack of wealth, and much more. Take control of your money, because if you don't, your money will take control of you.

Summary

Reaching your goals requires knowing

Where you are spiritually, mentally, socially, and emotionally,
Where you are going, and
How you will get there.

Management and Increase Proverbs can help you reach and maintain the appropriate balance financially.

Chapter 14 Seeking The Kingdom Of God

The theme of this book is found in Matthew 25:14 NKJV, which states, "For the kingdom of heaven is like a man traveling to a far country, who called his own servants and delivered his goods to them." Therefore, it would be safe to assume that to operate in the Kingdom of Heaven, one must seek the King to learn how His Kingdom operates (Matthew 6:33). By seeking the Kingdom of God, we use prayer, fasting, and scripture study to align ourselves with God's Will. There are three benefits to this alignment.

1) You will know God.
2) You will have proper perspective.
3) You will experience lack of worry.

You Will Know God

In referring to the master, the bad steward said, "I knew you to be a hard man" (Matthew 25:24 NKJV). The scripture teaches us the opposite in Matthew 11:30 NKJV, "For My yoke is easy and My burden is light." Had the lazy steward taken the time to know the master, he would have at least done as the master suggested in Matthew 25:27 NKJV, "So you ought to have deposited my money with the bankers, and at my coming I would have received back my own with interest." By knowing God, you will desire to do your best, and/or achieve the best outcome possible.

You Will Have Proper Perspective

The Good Stewards, after receiving their talents, went and traded with others. By seeking the Kingdom of God first, we align ourselves with proper perspective. For human beings, the perspective tends to shift at any given notice, or at best we focus on what we deem as priority at the expense of other things. By not seeking the Kingdom of God, we place whatever priority is dear to us first, which doesn't align us with God's Will. Therefore we are wasting our time. I experienced this first hand while writing this very chapter. My company was undergoing an audit, and my perspective immediately shifted from completing this chapter to audit preparation. Preparing for the audit wasn't wrong in itself, but not seeking the Kingdom for the direction I needed threw everything into chaos. Fortunately, through God's mercy, I was able to slow down, assess the situation, and seek the Kingdom of God for direction and proper perspective.

You Will Experience Lack of Worry

Worry is based on fear. In referring to the master, the lazy steward said, "And I was afraid, and went and hid your talent in the ground. Look, there you have what is yours" (Matthew 25:25 NKJV). In contrast, the good stewards were able to focus on the task at hand without worry or fear. By seeking the Kingdom first, we take our focus off of our worries.

In the previous example, I was so worried about the audit that I couldn't accomplish anything. Invoices relating to this book were misplaced; I even misplaced a portion of the manuscript itself! What was wrong with me? I forgot that when I sought the Kingdom of God first, all these things would be added to me. This meant guidance, peace, and solutions to all of my perceived problems.

I can't stress enough the importance of seeking first the Kingdom of God and His righteousness: "For what profit is it to a man if he gains the whole world, and loses his own soul? Or what will a man give in exchange for his soul?" (Matthew 16:26 NKJV). The soul can't be redeemed by riches. The Bible scripture teaches this in Psalm 49:6-8 NKJV, which states, "Those who trust in their wealth and boast in the multitude of their riches, none of them can by any means redeem his brother, nor give to God a ransom for him– For the redemption of their souls is costly . . . ." The Bible further expounds on this in Jesus' Parable of the Rich Fool found in Luke 12:15-21 NKJV.

v15 And He said to them, "Take heed and beware of covetousness, for one's life does not consist in the abundance of the things he possesses."
v16 Then he spoke a parable to them, saying: "The ground of a certain rich man yielded plentifully.
v17 "And he thought within himself, saying, 'What shall I do, since I have no room to store my crops?'
v18 "So he said, 'I will do this: I will pull down my barns and build greater, and there I will store all my crops and my goods.
v19 'And I will say to my soul, "Soul, you have many goods laid up for many years; take your ease; eat, drink and be merry."'
v20 "But God said to him, 'Fool! This night your soul will be required of you; then whose will those things be which you have provided?'
v21 "So is he who lays up treasure for himself, and is not rich toward God."

If money can't redeem a soul, then how is a soul redeemed? Only through God can a soul be redeemed. "But God will redeem my soul from the power of the grave . . ." Psalm 49:15a (NKJV). God has through God's mercy and grace extended this opportunity for redemption through God's Son, Jesus Christ.

Are you in need of redemption? The redemption of the soul is available by simply confessing with your mouth and believing with your heart that Jesus is the Son of the Living God and that God has raised Him from the dead. Thus shall you be saved. For with the heart one believes to righteousness, and with the mouth confession is made to salvation. If you have chosen to partake in this free offer, please repeat this earnest prayer to God with me:

Lord, I admit that I am sinner. I am sorry for all the sins I have committed against you and others. Please forgive me. I accept your forgiveness and believe that You (Jesus) are the Son of the Living God, and that you died for my sins. I believe that God raised you from the dead, and I ask that you come into my life as my Savior.

Some of you may experience feelings of relief and some of you may not, but rest assured that after you have sincerely prayed this prayer, you have received the gift of eternal life. Believe God, seek out a church which is biblically based, and embark upon your new life in God by studying the Bible. I recommend starting in the Book of John.

In closing, I sincerely hope this book has been a blessing to you, because it has been such to me. I pray that God will prosper you in all things and that you will be in health, just as your soul prospers. (See 3 John 2.)

Summary

Seeking the Kingdom of God leads to

Knowledge of God
Proper Perspective
Lack of Worry

Michael Fluker is a noted speaker and consultant based in Sarasota, Florida. He has appeared on local television talkshows and has been featured in several Christian magazines, including Westcoast Magazine, for which he writes an on-going column entitled "Money Matters". Michael currently lives in Sarasota with his wife, Julie.

If you are interested in having Michael Fluker conduct seminars at your church, conference, retreat, or organization, please contact:

Rhapsody Publications, Inc.
P.O. Box 991
Tallevast, FL 34270
941-866-1955
RhapsodyPublications@gmail.com

Visit RhapsodyPublications.net

Made in the USA
Monee, IL
04 November 2026

67381858R00115